THE LIFE OF GUY

The Life of Guy

GUY FAWKES, THE GUNPOWDER PLOT, AND THE UNLIKELY HISTORY OF AN INDISPENSABLE WORD

Allan Metcalf

OXFORD
UNIVERSITY PRESS

OXFORD
UNIVERSITY PRESS

Oxford University Press is a department of the University of Oxford. It furthers
the University's objective of excellence in research, scholarship, and education
by publishing worldwide. Oxford is a registered trade mark of Oxford University
Press in the UK and certain other countries.

Published in the United States of America by Oxford University Press
198 Madison Avenue, New York, NY 10016, United States of America.

© Allan Metcalf 2019

CIP data is on file at the Library of Congress
ISBN 978–0–19–066920–1

1 3 5 7 9 8 6 4 2

Printed by Sheridan Books, Inc., United States of America

Remember, remember the fifth of November,
Gunpowder treason and plot;
I see no reason why Gunpowder treason
Should ever be forgot!

Guy Fawkes and his companions did the scheme contrive,
To blow the King and Parliament all up alive.
Threescore barrels, laid below, to prove old England's overthrow.
But, by God's providence, him they catch,
With a dark lantern, lighting a match!

—traditional English poem

* * *

Nice guys finish last.

—Leo Durocher, manager, Brooklyn Dodgers

Nice guys may appear to finish last, but usually they are running a different race.

—Ken Blanchard,
author, *The One Minute Manager*

CONTENTS

Preface ix
Acknowledgments xi

1. Introduction *1*

2. Reformation *9*

3. The Original Guy *29*

4. The First Public Guy *53*

5. First Bonfire Day *66*

6. Gunpowder Days in England: The Pope and the Guy *74*

7. Pope Night in America: New World Guy *83*

8. My Pronoun, 'tis of Thee: Thou Art Lost and Gone Forever *91*

9. Guys in Rags *104*

10. Ladies and Gentlemen *115*

11. Roadblocks *125*

**12. Villain Becomes Hero:
The Modern Guy Fawkes** *137*

13. Guys Victorious *145*

14. Future Guys *150*

Further Reading: Notes on Sources *155*
Index *159*

PREFACE

This book is dedicated to you guys, who have turned the terrible name of England's greatest villain into a benign way of addressing family, friends, neighbors, colleagues, and the public in general.

It's a unique chapter in language history. "You guys" or simply "guys" is the only instance in the English language where the name of a person—and an evil terrorist at that—is now used by most of us as our second-person plural pronoun.

To get an idea of how strange this is, suppose we used a different name as our pronoun. Suppose it's Sean Connery, and we decide to make Sean our second-person plural pronoun. Everybody then would be addressed as Sean, as in:

> *Hurry up, you seans, look what's happening.*
> *My dear seans, whether you are 10 or 80, this applies to you.*
> *Your seans's mood needs a little improvement. Have a beer!*

Maybe a closer analogy would be to use the name of a modern villain like Osama bin Laden. We would then be saying things like:

> *Oh you osamas, how sweet of you to send me flowers from the whole group.*

> *Quiet, osamas! Listen to me. We can't win unless you give me your full attention. Hey, you osamas, did you hear what I said?*

But we don't use those names. Instead, we use the name of a terrorist so terrible that England still celebrates his defeat with bonfires and fireworks more than four centuries later.

How that came about is the story of this book. The story of Guy Fawkes's prominent front-line role in the Gunpowder Plot of November 5, 1605, is well known. So are reports of the Gunpowder Treason holidays decreed by Parliament for every November 5 thereafter. Language scholars know all about second-person plural pronouns. But no one seems to have noticed how remarkable it is that a hated name has unobtrusively turned into a benign word most of us use nowadays. Perhaps it helped that for centuries "guy" was such a slang word that nobody noticed its encroachment.

This book, then, puts it all together, showing how a hated name became the normal way to speak to any group of two or more in the 21st century.

ACKNOWLEDGMENTS

I alone am responsible for any errors in this book, but I have had help from many friends and colleagues in avoiding many mistakes.

Among them are linguists Michael Montgomery and Sali Tagliamonte, who helped provide the latest word on the spread of "guys." MacMurray colleagues who provided welcome help included Khara Koffel, Lucy Phelps, Susan Eilering and Gina Wyant.

Rita Salz told me about "guys" at Smith College in the 1950s, and Heather Williamson about the use of "yous guys" in the present.

Meanwhile, students at MacMurray College regularly offered reassuring unprompted evidence that "guys" was alive and well.

I appreciate careful review of the Guy Fawkes chapters by Fr. Kip Ashmore, and suggestions from Sara Metcalf and Kristen Chenoweth. And as usual, my wife, Donna Metcalf, posed significant questions that helped keep me on the right track.

At Oxford University Press, I was glad to work with Hallie Stebbins (now at Princeton University Press), Peter Ohlin, and Hannah Doyle, as well as production editor Alphonsa James of the affiliated Newgen Knowledge Works.

ACKNOWLEDGMENTS

THE LIFE OF GUY

1

INTRODUCTION

Terrorist becomes pronoun

Guy Fawkes enjoyed—or suffered from—a mere two months of fame before his life came to an abrupt and agonizing end. We know for certain that he died on January 21, 1606, when after a brief trial he was convicted of treason and publicly hanged, drawn, quartered, and beheaded.

But though he was dead, his legacy lives on in our language, until today it is stronger than ever. We call each other by his name.

Until the end of his life, Guy Fawkes was little known beyond his circle of family, friends, and colleagues. Coming from a good Catholic family in Yorkshire, England, he impressed others by his good looks and bearing, his manners, his courage, his devotion to duty, and not least his devotion to the Catholic faith. A tall, imposing gentleman, at age 35 he had earned a reputation for valor as a soldier fighting for the Catholic cause in the Low Countries, and known in particular for his expertise in placing gunpowder in tunnels to undermine and blow up enemy fortifications.

Back in England, on November 5, 1605, he had matches and fuses ready to apply to 36 barrels of gunpowder he had placed under the House of Lords in Westminster Palace, ready to blow it up with Lords, Commons, royalty, including King James I, and clergy present for the opening of Parliament.

He tried, and almost succeeded, to kill most of the government of England on that day. At the last moment, in the nick of time, he was discovered and prevented from lighting the gunpowder. Ever since, he has been viewed as the nation's arch villain, portrayed as a companion of the Devil himself.

But in his legacy, over the past four centuries things have changed. His name now lives more than ever, but with a change of heart. Though Guy Fawkes is unquestionably dead, his name is unquestionably alive in our language, nowadays more than ever before.

So guys, whoever and wherever you are, you are heirs of Guy Fawkes.

And "guys" means everyone, or nearly everyone, where English is spoken, especially in the United States outside the Old South.

It doesn't matter who you are—male or female; baby or child or teen or grown-up or past your prime; any race or place; athletic or lethargic; winner or loser—as long as you're a human being, you're one of the guys.

It is a remarkable fact, and yet not often remarked, that throughout most of the United States, indeed much of the English-speaking world, when we gather in groups we address the others as "guys" or "you guys." It's so normal nowadays that we scarcely notice how peculiar it really is: a singular "guy" referring to males only, alongside a plural "guys" including the entire human race.

So if a guy is speaking to a group of guys, we know that the speaker is male, but the audience can be male, female, or mixed, or for that matter GLBTQ: any person at all. If a female is the speaker, she's not a guy, but her audience of guys is still any person at all. And when that female speaker becomes a member of that same group but now is listening to someone else, she's one of the guys again.

In fact, "you guys" also now occupies territory at the heart of the English language, namely, the second-person plural pronoun. Though there are alternatives, most notably "y'all," those alternatives have retreated during the 21st century so far. Well, with an important exception we'll encounter later.

And never before in the history of the English language has any of the personal pronouns used a person's name.

But really, where did these guys come from? Yes, they came from Guy Fawkes, by strange twists and turns nobody could have imagined in 1605.

It will take a book to explain the unlikely circumstances that led to today's prevalence of guy and guys. So guys, pay attention. We can begin by pointing out a few highlights of the transformation from terrorist to innocuous informal greeting.

In America, ever since we declared independence and made a point of leaving the mother country's celebrations behind, we have pretty much forgotten the original Guy. That's important to the development of new meanings. England, however, still has memories of that particular Guy more than 400 years ago. In some places in England and the rest of the United Kingdom, they still burn a straw version of this Guy every November 5 on what is called Bonfire Night, Fireworks Night, or, more ominously, Gunpowder Treason Night.

Or, most ominously of all—and here's where you guys come in—Guy Fawkes Night. In January 1606, a grateful Parliament enacted the Observance of Fifth November Act, also called the Thanksgiving Act. November 5 hereafter would be a day of thanksgiving to God. It was to be a holiday, with church services in the day and bonfires and fireworks in the night, praising God for providential deliverance from gunpowder treason. With the day off, bonfires, and fireworks, November 5 immediately became one of England's top holidays.

Nowadays even in England, after more than four centuries, people often have to be reminded of the original Guy and what he stands for. But every November 5, shortly after we in the United States and many now in the UK have celebrated Halloween with costumes and trick-or-treating, some English towns and people still celebrate the narrow escape in 1605 of nearly the entire English government from the deadliest of bonfires and fireworks.

Historians have studied the English Reformation, the life of Guy Fawkes, and the Gunpowder Plot in great detail. Linguists have delved into the transformation of Guy into a name and then a pronoun. Language purists and language reformers have argued about the seeming sexism of a word that stands for everyone yet remains, in the singular, decidedly male. This book shows how they happen to tie together and aims to untangle the knot.

First things first, though. This book is not a biography of Guy Fawkes.

No, it's the story of a miracle, a transformation more miraculous than that of a caterpillar into a butterfly. The miracle indeed began with Guy Fawkes, but it has taken four centuries to accomplish, and neither he nor any of the other humans unwittingly involved in the transformation had any idea of the result now available to us in the 21st century.

And to occur at all, the transformation required many accidents of history involving characters and events as notable, and as remote from Guy Fawkes, as George Washington and the American Revolution.

The ample cast of characters involved in this transformation not only did not intend it but couldn't possibly imagine it. It was unimaginable because nothing like it had happened before, and it is highly unlikely that anything just like it will ever happen again. It deserves attention therefore not because it is a commonplace of human history and language but because it shows just how far out of the ordinary they can go. Truth is stranger than fiction.

True, it began with Guy Fawkes. If it hadn't been for his character, his participation in the plot to blow up the House of Parliament with legislators and royalty inside, and his near success in accomplishing that shocking act of total destruction, the miraculous transformation couldn't have begun. But thanks to his expertise in handling gunpowder, and to the fact that he was first to be caught, even though Fawkes was not the leader of the 13 conspirators, he was the leading figure in the eyes of the English government and public. That was where the miracle began. So his essential role in the transformation will require full attention in the chapters that follow.

At the same time, however, a full biography won't be necessary. For one thing, Guy has already been blessed, or more often cursed, with detailed biographies, such as Antonia Fraser's *The Gunpowder Plot: Terror and Faith in 1605* (2002), or one by John Paul Davis, *Pity for the Guy,* published in 2010. Both Fraser and Davis offer even-tempered judgments of both sides, in notable contrast to the generally vitriolic earlier treatments by authors who with their English compatriots saw Fawkes as a diabolical villain. That could easily be imagined by anyone thinking about the mayhem and loss of life Guy intended—and by the reminder, every November 5 since, of "the Guy's" murderous designs. But until that fateful moment, Fawkes himself was an honorable soldier, often involved in diplomatic missions, highly regarded by monarchs as well as by comrades in arms for his expertise and bearing.

But what is the miracle that calls for description and explanation? It is this: the transformation of a flesh-and-blood person into special kinds of words: the all-encompassing "guys," the masculine "guy," and a true linguistic miracle—a new second-person plural pronoun. And one that two centuries ago was nonexistent, one century ago exceedingly rare, but nowadays is both frequent and respectable.

"You guys!"

Granted, not everyone uses this second-person plural pronoun yet. And a few, though increasingly fewer, strongly object to it. But others who in the 20th century would have spoken up against it have now become comfortable with it—and even prefer it to older forms like you all or y'all, the abbreviated version that has served for more than a century as a marker of the "southern accent" in America.

For several centuries after the near-success of the Gunpowder Plot, "you guys" had nothing to do with pronouns. It was only after something also unprecedented happened to the pronouns of English that the use of "you guys" could be possible.

What happened to our language was that the old second-person singular gradually dropped out. Formerly, like German and Spanish and French and Italian, our language had both a singular (thou, thee, thine) and a plural (ye, you, yours) in what is called the second person, the pronouns we use in direct address to others. To this day those other languages keep this singular–plural distinction in the second person, but English does not. That also has an explanation, and it has to do with the character of English society.

Then came the American Revolution, another absolute necessity for the development of "you guys." Its role was to make

Americans gradually forget about Guy Fawkes. For the English, Guy was unquestionably an arch villain. But when Americans were also fighting a British government, the reasons and circumstances were quite different, so Guy was understandable as a heroic revolutionary.

Whatever you think of the concept of Intelligent Design, it doesn't apply to the development of "guys." True, there are many words whose origins can be traced to intelligent authors thinking rationally. The authors don't have to be divine, just humans wanting to frame their ideas more lucidly than the language has hitherto allowed.

But the process by which "guy" metamorphosed from one terrorist to a variety of everyday uses defies logic.

To see how it got from there to here, from then to now, we need to provide a fair amount of context. That means we must begin with the establishment of the Church of England, founded nearly a century earlier than 1605 because King Henry VIII wanted a divorce. The population of England was largely Catholic at that time. Soon the English church broke with papal Rome, and everyone was expected to renounce Roman Catholicism. Some resisted, and that begins the story of Guy and the guys.

2

REFORMATION

English religion gets a divorce

At the turn of the 16th century in 1500, the religious situation in England was simple. So simple, in fact, that it could be summarized in a single word. Catholic.

Not only that. Across the Channel in Western Europe, all other lands were also simply Catholic, all acknowledging the pope's supremacy. That was the way it was, and the way it had been for nearly a millennium and a half: Catholic, not by choice but because there was, in fact, no choice.

Within the wide embrace of the Catholic Church, of course, religious practices (and politics) were not the same everywhere. But the clergy, lords, and commons, in fact, just about everyone in England, were all Catholics. The civil wars conducted in England during the previous two centuries had been not religious but political, centering on the question of which descendants of King Edward III (1327–1377) should rule the country.

English Catholics in particular seemed to exceed expectations. Looking back on those times, a modern commentator noted that

> *The Church in England does a better than average job of keeping her clergy in good, honest order. Masses of pilgrims wend their way to the great shrines of Canterbury and Walsingham. Devotion to the Virgin is so great among the people that England is known across Christendom as the "Dowry of Mary."*

Taking religious unity for granted, therefore, no one in 1500, no matter how prescient, could have imagined the religious divisions and complications soon to follow. Still less could they have imagined that all these divisions and complications would arise, in part, from a king's determination to have his marriage annulled. But bizarrely enough, so it was.

Other religions trace their origins back to events like the creation of the universe, or the actions of gods, or at least to holy figures like Buddha, Jesus, or Muhammad. Some break off from established religions because of differences in doctrine. But the Church of England began because of a king's concern about his line of succession.

How that came about requires some explanation. And that, in turn, will begin to explain the complex context of conflicts that led to the Gunpowder Plot and then to our first *Guy*.

It goes back to the founding of the royal House of Tudor by King Henry VII in 1485. Victorious in battle, he decisively ended the Wars of the Roses by marrying Elizabeth of York and thus providing his progeny with ancestors from both York and Lancaster.

Fifteen years later, in 1500, all looked even better for King Henry and the Tudor dynasty. The peace had held. By 1500 Henry VII and Elizabeth had had eight children, including two stalwart princes, Arthur and Henry. As we have noted, the English rulers and people were still at that time, as before, Catholic.

Having founded a dynasty, Henry VII didn't leave the succession to chance. Just a few years after Henry VII became king, when heir apparent Prince Arthur was all of two years old, he was betrothed to Catherine of Aragon, a year older than the prince. Catherine was the daughter of Ferdinand and Isabella— yes, Columbus's Ferdinand and Isabella—so this wasn't a romantic love match but a political alliance intended to bring the kingdoms together.

In due course as planned, a little more than a decade later, on November 14, 1501, Prince Arthur and Catherine were married. Arthur was 15 years old and Catherine 16, now not only a great heiress but a renowned beauty. After only four months of marriage, however, Arthur died.

That wouldn't do. Still intent on the Spanish alliance, not to mention the beautiful Catherine and her dowry, Henry VII, lately widowed, offered to marry her himself. But Queen Isabella indignantly put her foot down. So Henry successfully negotiated with Spain for Catherine to be betrothed to Arthur's 10-year-old brother, Prince Henry, the new heir to the throne. Everything was back on track.

What does all this have to do with the Catholic Church in England? Nothing yet, except that the intended marriage required intervention by none less than the pope. Not a good sign.

This was the problem: Marrying a brother's widow ran into a difficulty declared in the Old Testament book of Leviticus:

> *None of you shall approach to any that is near of kin to him, to uncover their nakedness: I am the Lord (18:6). . . .*

> *Thou shalt not uncover the nakedness of thy brother's wife: it is thy brother's nakedness (18:16). . . .*

> *And if a man shall take his brother's wife, it is an unclean thing: he hath uncovered his brother's nakedness; they shall be childless. (20:21)*

True, those verses are seemingly balanced by Deuteronomy 25, which insists that a brother must marry the deceased brother's widow, if he left her childless:

> *If brethren dwell together, and one of them die, and have no child, the wife of the dead shall not marry without unto a stranger: her husband's brother shall go in unto her, and take her to him to wife, and perform the duty of a husband's brother unto her. (25:5)*

Still, the Leviticus strictures couldn't be ignored. Fortunately, everyone, including the pope, believed the pope could grant the couple dispensation from the admonition in Leviticus, and he did.

There were other difficulties, too, that have little bearing on the religious conflicts that later emerged. But finally by 1509 papal dispensation had been secured for Prince Henry's marriage to Catherine, and the dowry had been satisfactorily agreed on.

Henry VII died, presumably content, on April 21, 1509. Shortly after, on June 11, 1509, Henry VIII married Catherine. They exchanged these vows:

> *Most illustrious Prince, is it your will to fulfil the treaty of marriage concluded by your father, the late King of England, and the parents of the Princess of Wales, the King and Queen of Spain; and, as the Pope has dispensed with this marriage, to take the Princess who is here present for your lawful wife?*

Henry was nearly 18 years old and Catherine 23. So far, so good. England was still unquestionably Catholic. And Henry was happy with his beautiful wife.

Within a decade, however, an event and a movement occurred on the European continent that would complicate Western Christianity ever after.

In Germany, a monk named Martin Luther protested against certain practices of the Catholic Church—many practices, in fact—and their theological underpinnings. He famously nailed 95

theses to the church door at Wittenberg in 1517. For that chal-
lenge to papal authority he was excommunicated, charged with
heresy, and put to trial in Worms several years later. There he
refused to recant.

The rest is Protestant history. The pope kicked Luther out of
the Catholic Church by excommunicating him, but unrepentant
Luther turned the tables on the pope and kicked the Catholic
Church out of most of Germany.

But England? Not a chance, back then, that it would lose its
allegiance to the pope, or more specifically that Henry VIII would.
He not merely remained Catholic but became a fierce advocate of
the church's stance against Lutheran heresy.

In 1520, in a book whose attack on the pope bore the uncom-
plimentary title translated as "Of the Babylonian Captivity," Luther
disputed the Catholic doctrine of the sacraments. The church
maintained that there were seven sacraments; Luther argued that
only three, or maybe even two, met his definition of being bibli-
cally sacramental.

The theological debate between Luther and the church
electrified Europe. For our story, the details aren't relevant. What
is relevant is that Henry VIII, well-educated and energetic, vigorously entered the debate on the pope's side.

Henry wrote his treatise in Latin, of course, just as Luther and
any other serious theologian would. For as it happened, Henry
VIII had been given an excellent education in theology. His father,
Henry VII, intended his first son, Prince Arthur, to become king,
the secular ruler of England, and his second, Prince Henry, to

become archbishop of Canterbury, the head of the Catholic Church in England.

Henry had been a quick learner in all subjects, including languages and the sciences, and he was tutored in all of them, Catholic religion in particular. Because of Arthur's death Henry became king instead of archbishop, never taking religious orders, but he could dispute with the best of them, as his fearless attack on Luther shows.

Already in 1519, reading Luther's attack on the Catholic doctrine of indulgences, Henry had been moved to write a reply. This became the beginning of a fierce attack on Luther, published in 1521 and widely reprinted and circulated throughout Europe. Henry's book, published in 1521, was titled *Assertio Septem Sacramentorum adversus Martinum Lutherum*, translated as "Declaration of the Seven Sacraments Against Martin Luther."

The dedication of the *Assertio*, to the "Most Holy Father," reads like this in a conservative 1908 translation:

> *As We Catholic sovereigns should uphold religion, when We saw Luther's heresy running wild, for the sake of Germany, and still more for love of the Holy Apostolic See, We tried to weed out this heresy*
>
> *Seeing its widespread havoc, We called on all to help Us to eradicate it, particularly the Emperor and the Electoral Princes. Lest, however, this be not enough to show Our mind on Luther's wicked books, We shall defend and guard the Holy Roman Church not only by force of*

arms, but also by Our wits. And therefore We dedicate to Your Holiness Our first fruits, confident that an abundant harvest will be gathered, should Your Holiness approve Our work.

From Our Royal Palace at Greenwich, May 21st, 1521.

Your Holiness most devoted and humble son, Henry, by the grace of God King of England and France, and Lord of Ireland.

In defending the pope by arguing the Catholic positions on sacraments, indulgences, and other matters, including divorce, Henry does not mince words. Here is his concluding exhortation:

Do not listen to the Insults and Detractions against the Vicar of Christ which the Fury of the little Monk spews up against the Pope; nor contaminate Breasts sacred to Christ with impious Heresies, for if one sews these he has no Charity, swells with vain Glory, loses his Reason, and burns with Envy. Finally with what Feelings they would stand together against the Turks, against the Saracens, against anything Infidel anywhere, with the same Feelings they should stand together against this one little Monk weak in Strength, but in Temper more harmful than all Turks, all Saracens, all Infidels anywhere.

Cardinal Wolsey, Henry's permanent legate to the pope, commissioned several elegant illuminated manuscript versions of the *Asssertio* and selected the finest to be delivered to the pope. (To this day it remains in the Vatican library.) His Holiness was pleased with this vigorous, even vicious defense, more of an attack than a mere defense. So in October 1521 Leo X and his cardinals issued a bull awarding Henry VIII the title Fidei Defensor, that is, Defender of the Faith.

The bull awarding the title included this declaration:

> *Having found in this book most admirable doctrine We thank God and beg you to enlist like workers. We, the true successor of St. Peter, presiding in this Holy See, from whence all dignity and titles have their source, have with our brethren maturely deliberated on these things; and with one consent unanimously decreed to bestow on your Majesty this title, namely, Defender of the Faith. . . . We like wise command all Christians, that they name your Majesty by this title. . . . Having thus weighed . . . your singular merits, we could not have invented a more congruous name.*

Henry thus had become all the more explicitly Catholic, enabled by Luther's provocative treatises to clarify that he meant it in lucid theological detail. So with the century one-fifth over, England was still united as Catholic and loyal to the pope of Rome.

And so the years went by, happily enough at first. But Henry's worry about the succession increased. He needed a son, he thought; daughters were eligible for the succession, but in the history of England there had been only one daughter who actually became ruler, Matilda in the 12th century, and her tumultuous reign hadn't inspired confidence in feminine rule.

In any case, at first it appeared that his worry would soon - ended not long after Henry and Catherine were married in 1509. She gave birth to a son, named Henry, Duke of Cornwall, on New Year's Day 1511. All was well with this Henry for the first month and a half, but he died suddenly on February 22.

There was great mourning, but there was still plenty of opportunity for a male heir. His beloved Catherine, age 25 when the Duke of Cornwall was born, became pregnant many times after that, including with sons. But again and again they died from miscarriages or at birth.

In 1518, at age 33, Catherine became pregnant for the last time, once more giving birth to a son who died after just a day or two.

And Henry, well schooled in theology, began to worry that the curse of Leviticus 20:21 was exerting its force: "And if a man shall take his brother's wife, it is an unclean thing: he hath uncovered his brother's nakedness; they shall be childless."

Marrying your brother's widow prevented heirs, Henry gradually decided. Evidently neither Deuteronomy nor the pope could diminish that curse.

True, Catherine and Henry weren't quite childless. Their daughter Mary, born in 1516, grew to adulthood and qualified for the succession. Much later she did indeed rule England as "Bloody Mary," from 1552 to 1558. But for Henry only a son would do. Without a son ready to take the throne in proper succession, it seemed to Henry, the hard-fought unity of the Tudor dynasty might dissolve.

Maybe Henry needed another wife.

To get a new wife, however, he had to do something about his current wife. He knew well the church's position regarding marriage, which he had staunchly defended on behalf of his friend the pope. It was uncompromising.

As Henry had written in his *Assertio*, defending the sacrament of marriage:

> *What God hath joined together, let no man put asunder . . . . There must be understood sure something more holy than the care of propagating the flesh, which God performs in marriage ; and that, without all doubt, is grace; which is, by the Prelate of all sacraments, infused into married people in consecrating marriage.*

What to do? From long before that day, even to this, the Catholic Church has not countenanced divorce. Henry could hardly ignore that basic tenet of marriage, which he had himself endorsed with biblical authority.

For that matter, Henry needed something more drastic: not a divorce but an annulment, saying the marriage to Catherine had never taken place.

So he asked the pope, now Clement VII, to annul his marriage to Catherine.

Henry argued that the pope didn't have the authority to dispense with the Leviticus admonition against marrying a brother's wife, and so Henry's marriage to Catherine was not sanctioned, and so despite the solemn ceremony and all appearances, they had never been married. That would leave Henry free to marry young, fertile, sexy Anne Boleyn.

To say the least, Catherine was not pleased with that argument. Her defense was to declare that her marriage to Arthur had never been consummated, owing to the poor health that took the prince's life just four months after their marriage ceremony. That could be; it was unquestionable that she had not become pregnant by Arthur. If that marriage had not been consummated at all, Leviticus would not apply, and her marriage to Henry would have been her first and still entirely valid.

Nevertheless, Henry went ahead with his plan for domestic bliss and male succession. In 1531, Anne Boleyn began living openly with him. Toward the end of 1532, she became pregnant. They were secretly married in January 1533, well before the child would be born. In May, Thomas Cranmer, Archbishop of Canterbury, pronounced Henry's marriage to Catherine null, ensuring that their unborn child would be legitimate and putting the child at the head of the line of succession. Finally in September the child was born, a girl, named Elizabeth. Not the boy Henry was hoping for, but a good start all the same.

The pope, however, under pressure from the emperor of Spain, who happened to be Catherine's nephew (remember, she was from Aragon), wouldn't annul Henry's marriage. In fact, even if he wanted to, the pope couldn't, such was the pressure by the emperor, who literally laid siege to His Holiness's stronghold in Rome.

Frustrated, Henry tried pressure of his own. His "Reformation Parliament," summoned in 1529, followed Henry's bidding in transferring more and more authority in England from the pope to the king. First, in 1529, his Parliament abolished the separate religious courts that had given the pope jurisdiction over English clergy. The next year Parliament approved making it criminal to appeal to an outside power (in particular, the pope) for any English matter. They drastically reduced, and then eliminated, the church taxes paid to the pope, known as Annates, and also a household tax, known as Peter's Pence. Parliament, in support of Henry, had removed all papal authority and emolument from England and transferred them to the king.

In 1534 came the final step, Parliament's Act of Supremacy that made the king and not the pope supreme head of the church in England. The Act begins:

> *Albeit the king's Majesty justly and rightfully is and ought to be the supreme head of the Church of England, and so is recognized by the clergy of this realm in their*

> *convocations, yet nevertheless, for corroboration and con-*
> *firmation thereof, and for increase of virtue in Christ's*
> *religion within this realm of England, and to repress*
> *and extirpate all errors, heresies, and other enormities*
> *and abuses heretofore used in the same, be it enacted,*
> *by authority of this present Parliament, that the king,*
> *our sovereign lord, his heirs and successors, kings of this*
> *realm, shall be taken, accepted, and reputed the only*
> *supreme head in earth of the Church of England.*

It continues with more clauses enumerating the numerous ways he could assert his authority in every conceivable aspect of religion.

And so in 1533, assuming the authority bestowed on him by this Act of Supremacy, Henry VIII himself declared the annulment of his marriage to Catherine and his marriage to Anne instead. It was done.

Or was it? It's possible to imagine that after this little unpleasantness, and in the wake of this transfer of authority, England could have settled peacefully into a splendid almost-Catholic kingdom, with the only difference being that the pope had been replaced by the king as head of the established church. In such a situation, there would have been no possibility of a Gunpowder Plot in the next century.

But that's not what happened. Instead, the Act of Supremacy threw the door wide open to every sort of religious faction.

The Act of Supremacy took nearly 300 words to explain in painstaking detail the authority granted to the monarch and his successors. But it gave not the slightest indication of what kind of church the Church of England should be. It gave free rein to the king, who could change his or her mind about any religious practices at any time. And any subsequent king or queen would be free to follow, or just as free to disregard, the religious practices of his or her predecessor, as indeed proved to be the case.

But it also meant freedom of religion for the whole population of England. Or better expressed, freedom from obedience to the pope and the countless strictures and practices of the Catholic Church developed over the centuries. They were replaced, of course, by the strictures of the English monarch. But though the first English king to be recognized as head of the church was a gifted scholar, well read in theology and disputatious at that, he was too busy at first to bother about any religious matters except for Leviticus, enabling him to have his marriage to Catherine annulled in time for him to marry Anne.

As a result, numerous factions saw their chance to become the reformed version of the Church of England. Religious liberty is a modern notion; in the 16th century everyone, regardless of religious preference, took it for granted that the state would care for its subjects' souls by mandating religious doctrine and practice.

So what should that doctrine and practice be? Was it to be a continuation of Catholic practices, with the only change being the ultimate earthly authority? Was it to be just a little different from Catholicism, or as far from it as possible? Was it to be Lutheran, or Calvinist, or Puritan, or——? For in the wake of the Renaissance as well as Luther's challenges, England by the 1530s had many active religious factions, just waiting to be let loose. Books and pamphlets galore argued new religious views. In the midst of it in the 1520s came Tyndale's translation of the New Testament, influenced by (though not entirely sharing) Luther's views.

As long as Henry VIII was king, his new church would be whatever he wanted it to be. Not that he always wanted the same thing for it; politics and circumstances changed, and so did he. But anyone interested in promoting a particular religion knew that one thing was needed, one thing would remain uppermost: getting the king's attention and endorsement, then condemning all others as heresies insofar as they did not agree with the chosen way. And then doing all in one's power to induce the followers of false doctrine to abjure it and follow the true path, to avoid damnation.

Having only one authorized religion was nothing new. And having it imposed by the secular authority was also nothing new. So, for example, this was the way the Catholic Church had successfully converted England from paganism nearly a millennium earlier. Missionaries sent from Rome at that time made their arguments to the ruler and council rather than to the general population, knowing that the people would do what the king decreed. The Venerable Bede, England's first historian, gives this example:

After hearing Paulinus, one of the missionaries, make the case for Christianity to King Edwin of Northumbria in 627 A.D., the king's pagan high priest approved, declaring, in Bede's words:

> *Your Majesty, let us give careful consideration to this new teaching. For I frankly admit that, in my experience, the religion that we have hitherto professed seems valueless and powerless. . . . if the gods had any power, they would surely have favored myself, who have been more zealous in their service.*

Another counselor made another point:

> *Your Majesty, when we compare the present life of man with that time of which we have no knowledge, it seems to me like the swift flight of a lone sparrow through the banqueting hall where you sit in the winter months to dine with your thanes and counselors. . . . [Man] appears on earth for a little while, but we know nothing of what went before this life, and what follows. Therefore if this new teaching can reveal any more certain knowledge, it seems only right that we should follow it.*

The council agreed, the king approved, and King Edward's subjects all became Christians. That was the way it was done. For us in the 21st century, in first-world countries that no longer require everyone to adhere to the official religion, it's difficult to comprehend not only how serious a matter religion was in Guy Fawkes's day, but also how vicious.

Comparison with present-day religion in a democracy like the United States won't explain the harrowing religious conflict

Guy was born into. Americans indeed are free to choose their religion, not merely Catholic or Protestant but a smorgasbord of hundreds of varieties of Christianity as well as numerous other faiths beyond the Christian (or indeed atheism). They are guaranteed equal footing, and neither support for or opposition from the government, by the first part of the First Amendment to the US Constitution: "Congress shall make no law respecting an establishment of religion or prohibiting the free exercise thereof." To a 16th-century inhabitant of England, that would have been as incomprehensible as a declaration that the government would take no part in upholding the laws of the country.

Though Henry's assumption of supreme authority over the English church helped further complicate the formerly simple question of who should head a Christian church, it might be considered a step toward freedom of religion.

If so, it was just a little step, contested on all sides by those who universally agreed that the state had solemn sacred responsibility for the souls of its inhabitants. After all, what was more important than one's immortal soul? And so the devout Catholics and Lutherans and Puritans and others fought each other, often to the death and indeed beyond, starting at the time of Henry VIII. By the time of the Gunpowder Plot of 1605 the fighting had intensified, and for much of a half century after that it got even worse, until, finally, with the Restoration of the monarchy in 1660 after the extremes of Oliver Cromwell's puritan Commonwealth, tempers cooled enough to allow other religionists to coexist without threat of martyrdom. Even then it was another close to two centuries before Catholics were fully emancipated so that they could earn degrees from English universities and hold political office.

The extraordinary complexities and perils of religious life in England have been well chronicled by scholars and need not distract us further here. After Henry VIII died, England experienced extreme Protestantism for six years under his young successor Edward VI, full-blown Catholicism for the next five years under Mary, and finally for many years a kind of uneasy compromise, Protestant in authority but mixed Catholic and Protestant in practice. Protestant Puritans were almost as unhappy as Catholics with the Elizabethan compromise. Suffice it to say that in 1605 the greatest threat to protestant England remained the Catholics, since their allegiance to the pope challenged the foundation of the Church of England. The Catholic Church was the fundamental antithesis of the English. If the Catholics had succeeded in overthrowing the government, the English church would have vanished, swept into the dustbin of history.

Getting back to our prehistory of the Gunpowder Plot: Whatever else it became during the vicissitudes of Henry's whims and theological determinations, his church remained Protestant, that is, anti-Catholic, till his death in 1547. His son Edward VI, a staunch Protestant, reigned from 1547 to his death in 1553, making the church even more Protestant.

At that point a firmly Protestant church might have settled in and saved the country from much strife. But then Henry's daughter Mary, a staunch Catholic, ruled from 1553 until her death in 1558. During her brief reign she made England Catholic again, more extremely Catholic than ever before. She had many of the Protestant clergy who had led the English church under Edward burned at the stake.

And then Elizabeth came to the throne in 1558, reversing course once again, removing Catholics and restoring the Church of England. To people at the time it must have appeared that the Protestant–Catholic–Protestant reversals would continue indefinitely, leaving the people forever caught between opposing religions.

But it didn't work out that way, thanks to Elizabeth managing to rule nearly half a century, successfully foiling numerous plots against her. Since her legitimacy was not recognized by the pope, and indeed she was excommunicated by him, of necessity she was not Catholic. And though her church retained more Catholic features than most Protestant denominations, that wasn't enough for devout Catholics, who still kept allegiance to the pope.

As a result, the Gunpowder Plot shortly after her death was exceptional only in its extreme audacity. By 1605 there had been many plots against monarch and government, of increasing ferocity.

In other words, by 1605 Christianity in England had become so complicated as to almost defy understanding: not just by later historians but even more so by the contemporary players.

3

THE ORIGINAL GUY

Guy, Guido, John and the Plot

The circumstances that transformed a certain Guy into England's greatest terrorist began years before the near success of the Gunpowder Plot in November 1605. In fact, it could be argued that his destiny may have been determined on the very day he was born, April 13, 1570, when he was given the perfect name for an Englishman turned French villain: Guy Fawkes.

Guy was, and is, a distinctively French name, complete with the usual French pronunciation that gives it a vowel sound "ee" rather than "ay" after the hard G that begins the name—if it refers to a Frenchman, that is. The "guy" we use so often in our English conversation nowadays has the "ay" vowel, as did the "Guy" of the original Guy Fawkes, born and raised far from France in northern England.

Looking further back in time, that French *Guy* comes from a Germanic name *wido*, meaning either "wood" or "wide."

Guy had been firmly established as a familiar English name long before Guy Fawkes was born. The French-speaking Normans who conquered England in 1066 and then ruled for the next several centuries brought the name Guy with them and used it often. So it was by no means a rare or exotic name, just an English name that emphasized its Frenchness and its association with the ruling classes.

Perhaps most notable of the Guys in English memory was the legendary Guy of Warwick, a mostly mythical figure from long ago, comparable in prowess to King Arthur. Beginning as a humble page at the court of Earl of Warwick, in order to gain the hand of the Earl's daughter he embarks on heroic adventures. At first he kills the huge marauding Dun Cow and then a huge boar, making the neighborhood safe. Then he goes off to the Continent and gains the glory needed to make the daughter his wife, only to set out for the Holy Land, disguised as a pilgrim and encounters many more adventures. Very English, making Warwickshire his home, but still very French.

The distinctive French association with the name Guy has continued to this day. Probably the most notable of later Guys is the 19th-century French writer Guy de Maupassant, author of six novels and several hundred short stories. Meanwhile, the name Guy continues to be used for males born in England and America, like bandleader Guy Lombardo, Silicon Valley marketing executive

Guy Kawasaki, Pittsburgh Steelers football player Guy Whimper, and even the Muppet Guy Smiley along with numerous others, famous or not.

But to return to the 16th century, we find our particular Guy Fawkes: unquestionably an Englishman, born in York in northern England to a highly respectable family, but one that did not shy from its centuries-long association by name with France.

Later, during his long military career on the Continent fighting for Catholic Spain against the Protestant Dutch in the Low Countries, Fawkes started calling himself "Guido" rather than "Guy," perhaps to emphasize his religious distance from Protestant England. On his confessions under torture after his arrest, he signed his first name as "Guido." But he never tried to conceal his English birth and upbringing.

His one pseudonym, which he used only in the Gunpowder Plot, was by contrast ultra-English: John Johnson. Using that name he posed as a servant to Thomas Percy, a simple caretaker of the house Percy rented conveniently next door to that part of Westminster Palace where the House of Lords met. "John Johnson" was chosen for good reasons: It was English, it was common, and it was (in another sense) common. If you were looking for a name that sounded English, then or now, you would likely choose John, and then for good measure double it to John Johnson. Not a hint of French or any other foreign tongue there. If you were looking for a name that sounded familiar because so many bore it, again John would be a natural choice. It was the most popular name given to English sons born in the 16th and 17th centuries, and it has remained so ever since. It was nearly as anonymous as John Doe, the standard name given to an unknown party in legal proceedings.

And if you were looking for a name that suited a servant rather than a master, John would again be a good choice; it suggested the ordinary citizen, not a member of the nobility.

John Johnson was as close to being invisible as Guy Fawkes could have devised, a name ideally intended to evoke the least notice as Guy quietly went about his business in London. Perhaps he enjoyed the effect of the choice of his pseudonym, so distant from the distinguished name by which he had been known.

He was the first—and for a while the only—conspirator to be arrested, around midnight November 4 with damning evidence in hand. And with that he became immediately the focus of attention. He was promptly brought to the king's chamber for interrogation well before sunrise in that morning of November 5. There he openly admitted the Gunpowder Plot and its aim to restore Catholic rule to England. But he persisted in identifying himself as plain John Johnson, making that name an important part of his claim to know little about the conspirators.

If John Johnson really had been his name, or if he managed to keep that alias through all the interrogations that soon followed, instead of "you guys" might we nowadays be saying "you johns"? No. In that case, we would never have heard of either, and this book wouldn't exist. The developments deriving from the name Guy are unlikely enough as it is. But Guy is distinctive enough to serve, by odd chance, as the origin of a modern pronoun. John is not.

Like Guy, Fawkes was French in spelling and origin, but equally well established in English as a surname. It too was imported into England with the Norman conquest of 1066. Ancestry.com tells us that it derives ultimately from a Germanic name meaning "falcon." But say it aloud and it sounds like "fox," as some have interpreted it.

Like nearly everyone in England, Guy's English ancestors had been Catholic until Henry VIII's break with the Catholic Church in 1534. At the time of Guy's birth, and indeed even to the present day, despite strenuous efforts by rulers and governments many English people remained Catholic, except during the reign of Queen Mary (1553–1558), when Catholic affiliation and worship were strictly forbidden and punished.

So on April 13, 1370, that son was born to Edward and Edith Fawkes. On April 16, in the church of St Michael Le Belfrey in the center of York, he was baptized and given the name Guy. The newly renovated Belfrey was of course affiliated with the Church of England, as were all the authorized churches in the kingdom.

Guy's father, a lawyer, had to be a staunch supporter of the Church of England, since he served both the ecclesiastical and consistory courts of the Church in York, responsible for administration of church law. His mother, as far as historians know, presumably followed suit. She, however, had been a Catholic.

In the city and vicinity of York, numerous Catholics maintained the old faith, but it had to be in great secrecy, since Catholic "recusants" had to pay with fines and sometimes their heads for defying the government. The Church of England held all religious authority, and people had every inducement to accede to its authority. As for Guy, some of his relatives and connections in York were Protestant, some Catholic. But for his first eight years, he belonged to the Church of England.

When Guy was 8 years old, however, his father died, and his mother married another Catholic. Any Protestant–Catholic balance in the household came to an end. Guy was learning the Catholic way.

And the Catholic way, ever since Henry VIII proclaimed himself head of the English church, had been the way of uncompromising opposition. Often it was in secret, with increasing numbers of specially trained Jesuit priests being smuggled into England and protected by Catholic loyalists. Many an estate had a concealed "priest hole" to hide a Jesuit who would conduct Catholic services for the family.

Though by 1605 England had been Protestant for half a century, it had been Catholic for nearly a thousand years, and there remained plenty of secret Catholics who welcomed and supported Catholic attempts to regain the throne and overthrow the government.

In addition to the clandestine, however, there were numerous overt assaults on the Protestant government of England. The Gunpowder Plot was only the latest of them.

As we have noted in the previous chapter, Henry VIII's main contribution to the Church of England was simply to establish that its head was to be the English monarch rather than the pope. Exactly what the new Protestant practices should be was up for grabs. The rituals were by no means fixed, though they got a start with the Book of Common Prayer, compiled by Archbishop Thomas Cranmer and first published as the rule of faith and practice for the Church of England during the reign of Henry's young son Edward VI in 1549.

Within a few years, in 1553, Edward died and Mary took the throne, aggressively abolishing the Book of Common Prayer, restoring the Latin Mass that had been prohibited under Edward, banning the English-language Bible, and doing her best to make England Catholic once more. Three hundred Protestant clergy and lay people who had been leading the English Reformation under Edward were burned at the stake in an extreme effort to save their souls (and England).

Then came yet another abrupt turn of the wheel, Mary's death in 1558 leading to Elizabeth's succession. A revised Book of Common Prayer was issued in 1559. Catholics once again were ostracized, and the deadly Catholic–Protestant conflicts continued in earnest, with the shoe on the other foot.

Pope Pius VI in 1570 officially excommunicated Elizabeth, leaving little doubt which church she would have to support if she wished to remain queen of England. Not that there had been any doubt beforehand, but the pope's action made it certain.

In 1588, Pope Sixtus V repeated the excommunication. He proclaimed, in Latin of course:

> *First, for that she is an heretic and schismatic, excommunicated by two [of] His Holiness's predecessors, obstinate in disobedience to God and the See Apostolic, presuming to take upon her, contrary to nature, reason, and all laws both of God and man, supreme jurisdiction and spiritual authority over men's souls. Secondly for that she is a bastard, conceived and born by incestuous adultery, and therefore uncapable of the kingdom. . . . Thirdly for usurping the Crown without right. . . . The supreme Bishop. . . doth excommunicate, and deprive her of all authority and princely dignity, and of all title and pretension to the said Crown and kingdom of England and Ireland; . . . and absolving the people of those States, and other persons whatsoever, from all obedience, oath, and other band of subjection unto her, or to any other in her name.*

So many Catholic plots against Elizabeth were attempted, one after another, that contemporaries had to label them to keep them distinct. All failed, but some came close to ending her reign, generally by attempting to assassinate her and often with hopes for aid from Catholic Spain or France.

Among the most extreme were:

- *The Northern Rising of 1569, led by the Duke of Norfolk, with the aim of deposing Elizabeth and putting her cousin Mary, Queen of Scots, on the throne.*
- *The Ridolfi Plot of 1571, again led by the Duke of Norfolk, but named for a Florentine banker who acted as a go-between among Norfolk, the Spanish ambassador, and the pope. Spain would provide troops to invade England in support of the plot. Norfolk was executed.*
- *The Throckmorton Plot of 1581, named for Francis Throckmorton, who acted as go-between for Mary and another Spanish ambassador. This time French troops were to invade.*
- *The Parry Plot of 1584–1585 was supposedly the plan of William Parry, a Welshman in perpetual financial difficulty, to shoot the queen. He was a double agent for her and for the Catholics. Whether it was a real plot involving Sir Edmund Neville or an attempt to get Neville implicated continues to be debated. He got nowhere executing the plot and was himself executed.*
- *The Babington Plot of 1586–1587, named for Mary's page Anthony Babington, with the help of others, involved murdering Elizabeth to set Mary on the throne. Mary was in on this plot. She hoped Spain and France would help by invading England. The ambitious plan was doomed from its inception, however. Elizabeth's*

> devoted supporter Sir Francis Walsingham's clandestine network of
> spies monitored the plot from its inception, surreptitiously reading
> letters from the conspirators that were enough evidence to lead to
> their executions, including that of Mary.
>
> • *The Stafford Plot of 1587 would kill Elizabeth by blowing up
>   gunpowder put under the queen's bed. After this and the Babington
>   and so many other attempts to supplant her with Mary, Elizabeth
>   finally but reluctantly had Mary executed on February 8, 1587.*

Yet the plots kept coming.

> • *Most famous of all undoubtedly was the Spanish Armada, a fleet
>   of 130 ships that sailed in 1588 to bring Flemish troops to con-
>   quer England. A stout defense and worse weather destroyed that
>   attempt.*
>
> • *The Lopez Plot of 1594 was allegedly the intention of Roderigo
>   Lopez, the queen's personal physician, to poison her with the collu-
>   sion of Spain. He maintained his innocence, but Elizabeth had him
>   hanged. The existence of this plot remains a question, unlike all the
>   others.*

Most of the plots were by Catholics intending to restore the
Catholic faith in the kingdom. But there were others too, led by
unhappy people or factions within Protestant England. Most notably, in 1601 the Essex Rebellion, led by the queen's disgruntled
former favorite, ended with Essex's beheading.

Elizabeth's final years, ending in 1603, weren't pretty. Wars, taxes, bad weather, and harvests, even the Black Death in 1592–1594 made life challenging. And the plots went on and on, though none succeeded.

Despite lack of success, Catholics continued to plot as the 17th century began. Religion continued to be too important a matter to allow heresy to rule, whether heresy was defined as the Church of England or Catholicism, or even Puritanism, to make matters more complicated.

- *Again and again Catholics sought help from the king of Spain, now Philip III. In what became known as the Spanish Treason, in 1603 English Catholics sought funds from the king, as well as another Spanish Armada to conquer England. Philip expressed interest and sometimes encouragement, but nothing substantial developed.*

Here Guy Fawkes begins to enter the picture. Having made a name for himself over the past 20 years in the English Regiment of the Catholic Spanish Brigade that fought in the Netherlands, he was a member of the delegation sent to Spain in 1603 to persuade Philip to launch his invasion.

Meanwhile, as the queen's health deteriorated, Catholics and Protestants alike waited to learn whom she would designate as her successor. Elizabeth had used this tactic successfully throughout her reign, keeping various factions attentive and at bay by encouraging one and then another without indicating her preference—if indeed she had any.

Only on her deathbed in 1603, when she could no longer speak, Elizabeth signaled with her hands that James, for many years already King James VI of Scotland, would be her successor. At least that was the decision reported by those who attended her. After her death he was duly crowned James I of England on July 25, 1603.

The change of ruler encouraged Catholics to wait and see if James might exhibit more tolerance toward Catholics than his predecessor. His mother, after all, had been none other than Mary Queen of Scots, who had done her best for the latter part of her life to bring England back into the Catholic fold up to the point of losing her life for trying. Furthermore, James's wife, Anne of Denmark, had recently converted to Catholicism and maintained a friendly correspondence with the pope. She assured the pope that her children would be raised as Catholics and encouraged him to believe James would be tolerant of Catholics and Catholicism.

In a letter at that time to Robert Cecil, his secretary of state, James expressed himself in favor of such "diversity":

> *I will never allow in my conscience that the blood of any man shall be shed for diversity of opinions in religion, but I would be sorry that Catholics should multiply as they might be able to practise their old principles upon us.*

But like Elizabeth, James knew that his position as monarch depended on remaining Protestant as head of the independent Church of England.

- *And despite hopes of tolerance, threats of assassination did not cease. In James's inaugural year of 1603 he was the target of two somewhat related plots, simply called the "Bye Plot" and the "Main Plot." The inept Bye Plot, contrived by Father William Watson, was to kidnap James and hold him in the Tower of London until he fulfilled his promises of tolerance to Catholics. But then at the same time there was the Main Plot, this time a mainly Protestant revolt involving Puritans, the most extreme of the non-Catholics, yet at the same time seeking money from Spain to kill the king and his family so that the crown could go to Lady Arabella Stuart, whose religious affiliation was not so clear. Lady Arabella could then possibly marry a Catholic. We'll never know, because the Main Plot was foiled.*

James himself had been raised a Presbyterian in Scotland. But he differed from the Presbyterians and other Puritans in wanting a hierarchical church, with a system of bishops under overall authority of the monarch.

Seeing attacks from Catholics and Puritans alike, and an influx of Catholic recusants and priests from abroad with hopes of greater tolerance, James decided that tolerance wasn't the way to go. He chose instead to stay with the established Church of England, declaring much to the satisfaction of the defenders of the

English faith in February 1605 his "utter detestation" of the "superstitious religion" of the Catholics and that he was so far from favoring it that if he thought his son and heir would give any toleration to the Catholics, he would wish him fairly burned before his eyes.

So the momentary hopes for tolerance collapsed as the laws against Catholics were strictly and harshly enforced. And so came about the Gunpowder Plot, destined to be by far the most famous in the many decades of Catholic attempts to restore their faith. With the Gunpowder Plot, incidentally and quite unintentionally, began the sequence of events that led to "you guys" today.

Ever since it was undertaken and almost succeeded, the Gunpowder Plot has been associated in the public mind with Guy Fawkes. But the inventor of the plot and its unquestioned leader was a different man, Robert Catesby.

Catesby was a gentleman of some means and strongly Catholic background, of highly regarded character and military prowess, who had been involved in the Essex Rebellion against Elizabeth but escaped that occasion without punishment except for a large fine of 4000 marks.

When the new King James banished Jesuits and other Catholic priests and enforced the harsh fines against recusant Catholics, Catesby dreamed up his plot. But it was not just another in the endless series of Catholic plots aimed at dethroning a Protestant king by personally attacking the monarch or by sending an invading fleet or army. It was so outrageous that no one before Catesby had even imagined it, and so unimaginable it almost succeeded because the rulers and their spies and agents were not on the watch for it.

Catesby's plot was to be the grandest ever, several orders of magnitude greater than any previous ones. He figured out a way with one horrendous stroke to wipe out not only King James and his queen but the entire English government as well, including the Lords and Commons alike, the Privy Council, bishops of the Church of England, and senior judges, the latter all members of Lords.

How would this happen? Simply enough, with one horrendous stroke, by blowing up the House of Lords at the State Opening of the new session of Parliament, when all these dignitaries would attend in the presence of the king. The tremendous explosion would come from barrels of gunpowder hidden in the cellar under the House.

What would come afterward was more complicated and less certain. James's 8-year-old daughter Elizabeth, living elsewhere, would be kidnapped and put on the throne with a Catholic protector. And then, presumably, English Catholics would rise up in support of the plotters.

And then again, they might not. To attempt to kill the king and possibly a few others was one thing, and something the country had become all too familiar with ever since Henry VIII's break with the pope in the previous century. But to kill several hundred people, nearly all the government of the country? Even some of the plotters had their moments of hesitation.

But they also had their moments of fascination. One way or another, this audacious plot would go down in history over any others.

And so the plot took shape. As interrogation of the surviving plotters later revealed, Catesby first explained his awesomely simple plan to two others in a meeting at his London home in February 1604. As the time grew near, more were recruited and sworn to secrecy. All told, at the end there were 13 involved in the plot. To keep it secret, they involved as few as they could, but the logistics of placing 36 barrels of gunpowder under the House of Lords undetected required significant manpower.

Thomas Wintour, one of the three at that first meeting, later declared:

> He [Catesby] said that he had bethought him of a way at
> one instant to deliver us from all our bonds, and without
> any foreign help to replant again the Catholic religion,
> and withal told me in a word it was to blow up the
> Parliament House with gunpowder; for, said he, in that
> place have they done us all the mischief, and perchance
> God hath designed that place for their punishment.

The conspirators next met in a London suburb in May 1604. That time their number had grown to five. Before proceeding, the conspirators one after another swore this oath, holding a prayer book:

> *You shall swear by the Blessed Trinity, and by the Sacrament you now propose to receive, never to disclose directly or indirectly, by word or by circumstance, the matter that shall be proposed to you to keep secret; nor desist from the execution thereof till the rest shall give you leave.*

One of the newcomers recruited at this early stage and brought to this meeting was Guy Fawkes. Catesby needed someone experienced in underground explosions, and Fawkes was clearly the choice: a committed Catholic, a man of strength and probity and distinguished bearing, and one who had become an expert at using mines in warfare.

In the low marshy grounds of the Netherlands where the English Regiment fought on behalf of Spain against the Dutch Revolt, Fawkes had become skillful at destroying fortifications by undermining them with gunpowder. He had learned where and how to place a barrel of gunpowder effectively and how to connect it to a trail of slow-burning gunpowder called a train, or to a so-called slow match, that is, a rope soaked in limewater and saltpeter.

With the needed expert in charge, the work began. The House of Lords chamber was on the first level above a long disused basement. To prepare for the work of the miners, one of the conspirators, Thomas Percy, rented a house close to the House of Lords and installed "John Johnson," Fawkes's assumed name for the next year and a half, in the house, ostensibly as caretaker.

The State Opening was scheduled for February 7, 1605. That deadline put the conspirators to work in earnest. They had much to do to prepare for that date: digging the mine in the cellar, to begin with, and then bringing in the gunpowder, in barrels that would be large and difficult to hide as they were being delivered to the heart of London. (Some historians say, for complicated reasons, that this mining phase never happened. It wasn't essential to fulfilling the plot.)

It was only in October 1604 that they had all matters in hand: the rented house occupied by "John Johnson," adjacent to the House of Lords cellar and connected by a narrow path to the Thames River; barrels of gunpowder at Catesby's London house, to be delivered by night to the rented house; and workers to aid Johnson in siting and preparing the explosives.

Further delay was caused by unexpected difficulties in leasing the house. Not until shortly before Christmas could the actual mining begin.

Even so, the work went slowly. Right next to the seat of government wasn't the easiest location to conduct such a major operation in total secret. Amazingly, they did so during all the preparations, probably because the idea of blowing up the House of Lords was, as mentioned before, unthinkable—to anyone aside from Catesby and the conspirators he recruited and swore to secrecy. It's even possible that a spouse or friend of the plotters, hearing an inadvertent mention of an aspect of the plan, would have dismissed it as unthinkable. Whatever the reasons, the secret remained intact.

And then there was the matter of the cellar. True, it was unused, undisturbed, and uninspected by the authorities, but the cellar walls happened to be nine feet wide, as well as nine feet tall, and made of brick. That's a lot of mining to make room for lots of barrels of gunpowder.

But they went to work in earnest: a crew of five gentlemen, listed by biographer John Paul Davis as "Wintour, Guy, Catesby, Wright and Percy." As a modern-day guy, Davis uses Fawkes's first name un-self-consciously, while referring to the others conventionally by their last names.

Whether they would finish in time for the State Opening in February soon became a moot point, because it was postponed further, till October 3, 1605, on account of the plague.

And in March 1605 they had unexpected luck. Near where they were working, the men heard noises that sounded something like shoveling coal. Fawkes went to investigate and found that indeed, coal was being shoveled. A coal merchant had rented a spacious vault right under the House of Lords and was now removing the coal. Percy immediately arranged to lease that space, and from then on the work was much easier: no digging required, just moving the barrels of gunpowder to a more effective location than originally chosen.

To move that much material inconspicuously still wasn't easy, but they did so that spring and summer of 1605 without further complications. In case the authorities should investigate, they covered the barrels with wood—supposedly firewood for Percy's house.

From time to time, as needed, an additional conspirator would be added. All told, there would eventually be 13. In addition to Fawkes, Catesby eventually had recruited John Wright, Thomas Wintour, Thomas Percy, Robert Keyes, Thomas Bates, Robert Wintour, Christopher Wright, John Grant, Ambrose Rookwood, Sir Everard Digby, and Francis Tresham.

We generally refer to them by their last names, of course—all except Guy Fawkes. At first, once he shed the alias John Johnson, the man called "Guido" in Europe confessed to his real name, and he was normally referred to in official proceedings by his last name, like all the others. It was not until some years after the plot was prevented and Parliament issued orders to celebrate the country's deliverance with bonfires that he generally became spoken of as Guy.

The State Opening had one final postponement, from October 5 to November 5. The delay made Fawkes worry whether all the gunpowder already in the vault would work. So to be sure, he bought more. He had made a trip to France that summer for fresh dry powder. All told, on the eve of the State Opening there were 36 substantial containers of various kinds—technically not just barrels but also firkins and hogsheads—ready to be exploded in the morning of November 5.

Meanwhile, the king and his ministers had finally learned that some sort of trouble was in the works. The tip came from Lord Monteagle, a friend of Catholics but also of the king, who received an anonymous letter on October 23, warning him "as you tender your life to devise some excuse to shift off your attendance at this parliament. For God and man have concurred to punish the wickedness of this time. . . . For though there be no appearance of any stir, yet I say they shall receive a terrible blow this parliament. And yet they shall not see who hurts them."

Sir Robert Cecil, the king's secretary of state and spymaster, was promptly informed and prepared to take action. But there was little indication of what the danger to the Parliament would be.

In England, as elsewhere in the northern hemisphere, November is a dark time of year. Even in London. Perhaps especially in London, since the capital city had the tallest buildings in the country, and the closest together. Nowadays when the sun sets there on a November day, the lights of the city go on. But in 1605, of course, there was not a single electric light. Torches and lanterns were the best they could do, and they didn't drive much of the dark away.

In the dark night of November 4, 1604, the London sun set early. If there was a royal astronomer paying attention, and if it wasn't too cloudy, he could note the slanting sun set at 3:52 p.m., though he wouldn't have expressed it that way or so precisely. It was Tuesday by the old-style calendar then in effect, Saturday by the new one that was adopted more than a century later. Sunrise would come at 7:49 a.m. after a night unlike any England has ever experienced before or since.

So it all came down to this night. Moving quietly through the familiar dark narrow streets near the Houses of Parliament, a tall, athletic, dark-clad figure arrived once more at the house next to the House of Lords. If the night watch noticed him, they paid him little heed, since he had been a familiar figure in that neighborhood for well over a year.

Who was this man? None other than Guy Fawkes, alias Guido, alias John Johnson, unknown to the nation as yet, but destined before dawn to become one of the most memorable figures in English history.

Fawkes looked around at the silent street. Then, satisfied that no one he knew was in sight, he slipped in the door and went to work. Fawkes put the final touches on the fuses connecting to the barrels. He had touchwood and a tinder box in his pockets to light them—with a new pocket watch from Percy to properly time the lighting.

They were very slow-burning fuses, and for good reason; Fawkes needed to get far away before such a powerful explosion. He wore boots and spurs, ready to make a quick exit.

Satisfied that everything was ready, he left for a while. When a search party sent by Cecil entered the cellar and looked around, they noticed a tall, rough-looking man along with unremarkable piles of wood. They felt something suspicious about the situation, but they couldn't find out. So they left without arresting the man or uncovering anything else.

But a second search party was sent to inspect once again. This time, shortly after midnight on November 5, they found the man still there and arrested him. Searching his pockets, they found the touchwood and tinder box and confiscated them.

There would be no explosion after all.

Present-day scientists have been curious about how powerful the explosion would have been and what damage it would have caused if Fawkes had succeeded in setting it off. Supposing all the gunpowder in those 36 barrels had been dry and ready to blow, members of the British Institute of Physics in 2003 figured that the roughly 2.75 tons of gunpowder would have destroyed not only the House of Lords but most buildings within a radius of about one-third of a mile, including the rest of the Palace of Westminster. That would be about 25 times as much explosive as needed. The BBC quoted researcher Catherine Gardner of the University of Wales as saying, "There is a possibility that the Houses of Parliament and Westminster Hall would have been completely obliterated, although we can't know for sure."

And so the worst terrorist attack in the history of England never happened after all. It could even be argued that it might have been the worst terrorist attack in the history of the world. Many lives have been lost at one blow in other attacks, of course, like that of September 11, 2001, at the World Trade Center and the Pentagon. But no other attack would have taken so much of the government of a country.

It is with such a possibility in mind, perhaps especially this Gunpowder Plot, that since the 1960s a lower-ranking Cabinet member is selected to stay far away from the US Capitol during the president's annual State of the Union address. Everyone else in the government assembles for that occasion in the House chamber: the full membership of the House and the Senate, the

Supreme Court, the rest of the Cabinet, and other high officials. The Cabinet member who stays away is called the "designated survivor," who would be next in line to serve as president if those at the State of the Union were destroyed. It isn't likely to happen, but the premise has become a successful television series featuring Kiefer Sutherland.

If the Gunpowder Plot had succeeded, it is possible to imagine that world history might have been changed. For example, the North American continent might have become part of Latin America as Spain, after the explosion, accepted an invitation by English Catholics to occupy the country. Or maybe not; the devastation of the ruling classes might have been so stunning that many English Catholics would have had no sympathy for the plotters.

But by good luck or good detective work, it didn't happen. The terrorist plot was stopped before the fuses were lit for 36 barrels of gunpowder in the ground-level cellar under the Houses of Parliament. And so instead of instigating regime change, what became known as the Gunpowder Plot instigated language change, big time.

4

THE FIRST PUBLIC GUY

Interrogation, identification, trial and public execution

The House of Commons Journal for November 5, 1605, records:

> *This last Night the Upper House of Parliament was searched by Sir Tho. Knevett, and one Johnson, Servant to Mr. Thomas Percye, was there apprehended, who had placed Thirty-six Barrels of Gunpowder in the Vault under the House, with a Purpose to blow the King, and the whole Company, when they should there assemble.*
>
> *Afterwards divers other Gentlemen were discovered to be of the Plot.*

On that first fifth day of November, immediately after the arrest of "John Johnson," nobody at court connected him with a guy named Guy. And so it continued for two full days (November

5 and 6) while the man they first arrested maintained his identity as Johnson. On the third day, weakened by increasing torture, he admitted to being Guy Fawkes—or should it be Guido, his Continental version? He chose Guido when he signed his name with a shaky hand on the pages of the transcript of his interrogations.

But it was "John Johnson" who was arrested very early on November 5. He was brought directly to the bedchamber of King James for questioning at about four in the morning,"Johnson" maintained his fabricated name and history. He was then brought directly to the prison cells of the Tower.

After that early-morning interrogation, James was sufficiently concerned that he himself drew up a list of 16 questions to be asked of the prisoner. "Ask what he is," he began, "for I can never yet hear of any man that knows him."Then there are:

> *13. What Gentlewoman's Letter it was, that was found upon him?*
> *14. And wherefore doth she give him another name in it, than he gives to himself?*

On the afternoon of November 6, those questions were put to him and he gave answers. Apparently they didn't do much good. The letter, from a woman supposedly named Bostock, never was made public.

The handwritten report of his interrogation includes matters like these:

*He saith, that he knows not but by generall report and
by making ready of the kings barge, that the king was
coming thither the first day of this parliament, But
confesseth that his purpose was to have blowne upp the
upper house whensoever the king was there.*

*And being demanded when the king, his royal issue,
the Nobles, Bishops, Judge, and of the principall of the
Comons, were all destroyed what government would have
ben, Answereth we were not growne to any determination
therein, and beeing but a fewe of them the could not enter
into such conforsation, but that the people of themselves
would decide a head. . . .*

*He confesseth that he hath knowne Mr Percy two or
three years but served him not, but about three moneths
before the house was hired as is aforesaid,*

*Being demanded what noble men were warned, that
they would not be there at that time, Answereth, wuld
durst not forewarn them for feare wich should be discovered, And being asked why he would be a partie to
any acte that might destroy any that was of his owne
relligion, Answereth, we meant principally to have
resported [respected] somme safely, and would have
prayed for them.*

As an explosives expert, happy to display his expertise in
blowing up enemy buildings and fortifications, the prisoner apparently needed little coaxing to reveal the technical aspects of the

plot. But he refused to name his co-conspirators. Or, rather, he said he didn't know who they were. After all, he was just plain old John Johnson, servant to Thomas Percy. So the official Calendar of State Papers records for November 6, adding the true name in parentheses as it had come out that day:

> *Examination of John Johnson (Guy Faukes) as to the storing of powder, &c. in the Parliament cellar,——his connections abroad,——whether Mr. Percy would have allowed the Earl of Northumberland to perish, &c. He refuses to inculpate any person, saying, "youe would have me discover my frendes: the giving warning to one overthrew us all;" signed "John Johnson."*

That day "John Johnson" continued to explain the intention of the plotters but would still not give their names—or reveal that his was a pseudonym. So King James issued these instructions: "If he will not otherwise confess, the gentler Tortures are first to be used unto him and so by degrees proceeding to the deepest." Or in the original form in Latin as well as English:

> *The gentler tortours are to be first usid unto him, et sic per gradus ad ima tenditur, and so God speede youre goode worke.*

Torture was a rare tactic, requiring approval of the king, and reserved for serious crimes.

The first of the "gentler" tortures was iron gauntlets to hold his arms shackled to a wall. To gradually stretch him and increase the pain, the gauntlets could be raised and the wooden supports he stood on could be removed. "Johnson," however, remained quiet with calm resolution for a whole day and evening of torture, and slept peacefully at night.

Still, resolute as he was, he could not hold out forever. The official record for November 7 indicates that he finally admitted to being Guy Fawkes, known on the European Continent as Guido. And he named the other conspirators. Once again the Calendar of State Papers:

> *Examination of Guy Faukes. The conspiracy began eighteen months before; was confined to five persons at first, then to two; and afterwards five more were added, who all swore secrecy; he refuses, on account of his oath, to accuse any; they intended to place the Princess Elizabeth on the throne, and marry her to an English Catholic. Signed at the foot of each page "Guido Faukes."*

King James issued a stern proclamation, printed and widely distributed on November 7, naming Percy, telling the plot, and commanding

> *our Lieutenants, Deputy Lieutenants, Sheriffes, Justices of Peace, Mayors, Bayliffes, Constables, and all other our officers, Ministers, and loving Subjects, to . . . employ*

> *themselves for the suppressing, apprehending, deterring,*
> *and discovering of all sorts of persons any wayes likely to*
> *be privie to a Treason so hatefull to God and man.*

The proclamation then names Percy and concludes with names of seven other conspirators. It doesn't mention Fawkes, probably because he had already been apprehended.

On the morning of November 8, still frustrated, the director of the interrogation, Sir William Waad, lieutenant of the Tower, reported to his supervisor, Sir Robert Cecil, Earl of Salisbury and Secretary of State:

> *My Lord,*
>
> *I do think it my duty to give your Lordship daily ac-*
> *count of what temper I find this fellow, who this day is*
> *in a most stubborn and perverse humour, as dogged as*
> *if he were possessed. Yesternight I had persuaded him to*
> *set down a clear narration of all his wicked plots, from*
> *the first entering on the same to the end they pretended,*
> *with the discourses and projects that were thought upon*
> *amongst them, which he undertook to do, and craved time*
> *this night to think him the better. But this morning he*
> *hath changed his mind, and is so sullen and obstinate as*
> *there is no dealing with him.*

But as strong and strong-willed as Fawkes was, he could not withstand another day of torture. So the daytime interrogation on November 8 got him to reveal just about everything. That day's Calendar recorded:

> *Deposition of Guy Faukes. Thos. Winter first proposed a*
> *conspiracy to him; Catesby, Percy, and John Wright were*
> *next taken into the scheme, then Chris.Wright, afterwards*
> *Sir Everard Digby, Amb. Rokewood, Francis Tresham, John*
> *Grant, Rob. Keyes, and many others. Details of the Plot,*
> *the same as in the examinations.*

His stubborn refusal at first to name names, even under torture, impressed his captors. If he had held out till he died, it is conceivable that the other perpetrators of the Gunpowder Plot would never have been discovered.

But he had already let one big cat out of the bag. The moment he was arrested, he gave the name of his supposed employer, Thomas Percy, cousin of the Earl of Northumberland. That led to a search for Percy, which then led to all the rest.

Already in the light of day on November 5 a proclamation had been issued for the apprehension of Percy. The king's broadside proclamation of November 7 added half a dozen names to the search.

The hunt for the rest of the plotters put the country in turmoil, but Guy's resistance to torture gave them a head start. Counting Guy, there were 13 conspirators, and all but Guy were still at large for a few days after his arrest. Most of them had been in London, but all succeeded in escaping the city.

Finally on November 8 the sheriff of Worcester, with a posse of 200 men, caught up with a majority of the fugitives at Holbeche House in Staffordshire, more than 100 miles west of London. Four were killed in a shootout there: Percy, Catesby, John Wright, and his brother Christopher Wright.

Five others were captured at Holbeche or nearby that day: Catesby's servant Thomas Bates, John Grant, Ambrose Rookwood, Sir Everard Digby, and Thomas Wintour. Robert Keyes was also arrested that day. All were of course delivered to the Tower of London, and they had additional information to be extracted, but until they arrived Fawkes was the only conspirator available to the authorities.

Interrogation of Thomas Wintour began November 12. Francis Tresham was captured November 12. He died, supposedly of natural causes, on December 23.

The last two fugitives, Thomas Wintour's brother Robert and Stephen Littleton, were captured on January 9, 1606.

Catesby, the inventor and director of the plot, would undoubtedly have been the primary focus of government attention if he had been available. But since he had been killed before the authorities could get to him, four centuries later we say "you guys" instead of "you robs."

In the days that followed, the story of the plot and its characters became widely known. And the point man who had been ready to light the gunpowder and then ride quickly away, who had held out against torture to an extent that amazed his captors, and who also was known for his stalwart soldierly bearing and expertise, in addition to being red-headed, well dressed, and more than six feet tall, drew more and more attention. Guy was on his way to being the very different guy we know today.

As Guido, his name continued now and then to appear, for example at the end of a 1606 book reporting His Maiestes Speech in This Last Session of Parliament:

> *The Trve Copie of the Declaration of Guido Fawkes, taken in the presence of the Counselllers, vvhose names are vnder vvriten.*

But Guy, the name we are looking for, was becoming well known, even better than Guido, soon after November 5. In a sermon preached at Paul's Cross on November 10, the Bishop of Rochester declared,

> *So ment Guy Faulkes (the true name of a false traytor) to haue beheld as (hee said) the houses and bodies flying vp; he liuing & laughing at it If hee had solde vs for bond-slauos & hand-maides, saith Hester of Haman, yet there had been life, and so hope of returne, but to make an vtter dissolution of the whole State, had beene a misery incurable, was a proiect most damnable.*

Another variant, ingeniously combining the English and Continental versions of the arch-villain's names, appears in a 1606 printing of Thomas Nash's *The returne of the knight of the poste from Hell with the diuels aunswere to the supplication of Pierce Penilesse, with some relation of the last treasons.*

> *But (sayd he) Deuils me no denils, they may hereafter through iudgement proue Deuils, but as yet they are men, which both contriude, and should haue executed: Haue you, (quoth I) heard any of their names—their names (replied he) why: I am of familiar acquaintãce with them all, he that should haue executed, and was like wise a contriuer, was one Guy do Faulkes.*
>
> *The especial Plotte-layer, was Thomas Piercy, Robert Catesby, the two VVinters, John VVright, Christopher VVright, and diuers others: truely (aunswered I) you doe but delude me, for these fellowes, were of such vnder qualitie, and so farre from hope of aduancement, by the subuersion of the common-wealth, that except all gentrie should be rooted out, and nothing left but their families: I see not which way they should haue raisde their fortunes one steppe higher: as for Faukes I neuer hearde his name before.*

The trial of the eight living conspirators on January 27 gave further notoriety for the man now usually referred to as Guy Fawkes. The official record of the trial, more than 11,000 words long, exclusively used that form of the name and that spelling. It began in the heading:

XIX. The Trials of Robert Winter, Thomas Winter, Guy Fawkes, John Grant, Ambrose Rookwood, Robert Keyes, Thomas Bates, and Sir Everard Digby, at Westminster for High-Treason, being Conspirators in the Gunpowder-Plot. 27 Jan. 1605. 3 Jac. l.

And continued in the full list of conspirators, repeated again and again, in the indictment:

Guy Fawkes Gent. otherwise called Guy Johnson . . .

. . . the said Henry Garnet, Oswald Tesmond, John Gerrard, and other Jesuits, did maliciously, falsly, and traitorously move and persuade as well the said Thomas Winter, Guy Fawkes, Robert Keyes, and Thomas Bates, as the said Robert Catesby, Thomas Percy, John Wright, Christopher Wright, and Francis Tresham. . . . To which traitorous Persuasions, the said Thomas Winter, Guy Fawkes, Robert Keyes, Thomas Bates, Robert Catesby, Thomas Percy, John Wright, Christopher Wright, and Francis Tresham, traitorously did yield their Assents: And that thereupon the said Henry Garnet, Oswald Tesmond, John Gerrard, and divers other Jesuits; Thomas Winter, Guy Fawkes, Robert Keyes, and Thomas Bates, as also the said Robert Catesby, . . . traitorously amongst themselves did conclude and agree, with Gunpowder, as it were with one Blast, suddenly, traitorously and barbarously to blow up and tear in pieces our said Sovereign Lord the King. . . .

> . . . *the said Guy Fawkes, afterwards, . . . traitorously*
> *had prepared, and had upon his Person Touchwood and*
> *Match, therewith traitorously to give fire to the several*
> *Barrels, Hogsheads, and Quantities of Gunpowder afore-*
> *said, at the time appointed for the Execution of the said*
> *horrible Treasons.*

All told, this record used Guy Fawkes 21 times, plain Fawkes another 14 times, but no Guidos. Guy was becoming well known.

It was no surprise that the jury found all the defendants guilty. King James graciously gave them only "an ordinary Punishment, much inferior to their offence," since they "exceeded all others their Predecessors in Mischief, and so Crescente Malitia, crescere debuit & Pæna." Ordinary punishment for traitors was to be hanged, drawn, and quartered, and so they were on January 30 and 31. The last to be put to death was Fawkes, who managed to die from hanging, his neck broken, so he was not conscious for the rest of the indignities to his body.

If John Johnson really had been his name, or if he managed to keep that alias through all the interrogations that soon followed, instead of "you guys" we might nowadays be saying "you johns."

Not!

The other names wouldn't have served to develop into 21st-century pronouns—John too common, Guido too foreign and esoteric. But Guy—that's a plain guy well suited for commando duty in the structure of English. He successfully infiltrated the English language even as he didn't manage to successfully command the cellar under the House of Lords.

5

FIRST BONFIRE DAY

Fires on the Fifth of forever

Among the many plots against the monarchy and government following Henry VIII's audacious act removing the English church from the pope's authority to his own, none was so unanticipated and horrendous as what became known as the Gunpowder Treason. It was horrifying to imagine what would have happened to the country if practically the whole government had been destroyed all at once by an enormous explosion that would literally bring down the house. Perhaps it was all the more horrifying that it was foiled at the last moment, since it left everyone free to imagine the worst.

If there had been an actual explosion, it might not have been as powerful as one might imagine. As a scientific experiment early in the 21st century conclusively proved, there is no question that if all 36 barrels had been dry, the explosion would indeed have blown the House of Lords to bits and killed everyone in it. But it is also quite possible that some of the barrels would have been too wet to explode. That seems to have been the plotters' motivation for taking the time and effort to bring in an additional 16 barrels after the first 20 had been installed.

In some ways it was like Osama bin Laden's astonishing attack on the World Trade Center and the Pentagon on September 11, 2001, by an unprecedented means that was totally unforeseen by anyone in America even though authorities had been monitoring terrorist activities for years. The difference was that bin Laden and his Al-Qaeda almost completely succeeded, while Catesby and his Gunpowder Plotters were utterly foiled.

In bin Laden's case, one of the four hijacked airplanes was prevented from hitting its target by the efforts of its passengers. That left everyone free to worry and speculate: Would it have been headed toward the White House? Or another vital or symbolic target?

In Catesby's case, English Protestants could speculate unchecked, understandably imagining their darkest fears of Catholic uprisings. Who knows what would have happened afterward?

The fleeing Gunpowder Plotters looked for support from spontaneous uprisings of recusant Catholic supporters, and perhaps an invasion from Spain or France, or maybe a personal appearance by the Devil himself—anything might have been possible. Or there might have been an all-out civil war.

But there was also great jubilation in England when news of the plot was accompanied from the very beginning by news of deliverance. It was a matter for fear but even more for rejoicing. To the king and most of the population, even some recusant Catholics, it seemed a manifest sign of God's favor, especially to the Church of England. All the more the feeling grew as days went on, as every one of the plotters was killed or arrested, and those arrested were tried, convicted, and put to a traitor's public death. Everyone involved in the Gunpowder Plot was dead and gone before the end of January. The victory over unthinkable evil was complete.

On November 5, 1605, celebrating news of the defeat of the Gunpowder Plot, the population of London lit up the city with bonfires, cheerful tokens of the terrible explosion Guy Fawkes intended. It was an occasion to remember, but also one that might have faded from memory, or at least from celebration, in a few years. By the end of January the next year, all of the plotters were gone for good, and the celebrations might have gone too.

That didn't happen, however, because of the "Observance of Fifth November Act," more formally titled "An act for a publick thanksgiving to Almighty God every year on the fifth day of November."

It was introduced to the House of Commons in Parliament on January 23, 1606, and approved two days later. It explains:

> *many malignant and devilish Papists, Jesuits and Seminary Priests, much envying and fearing, conspired most horribly, when the King's most excellent Majesty,*

> *the Queen, the Prince, and all the Lords Spiritual and*
> *Temporal, and Commons, should have been assembled in*
> *the Upper House of Parliament upon the Fifth Day of*
> *November in the year of our Lord One thousand six hun-*
> *dred and five, suddenly to have blown up the said whole*
> *House with Gunpowder: An Invention so inhumane, bar-*
> *barous and cruel, as the like was never before heard of.*

Backed by the parliamentary mandate, the celebration soon burst into prominence in the English calendar of feasts. It had everything, high and low: sermons and prayers in solemn religious services of thanksgiving, on the one hand, and bonfires and fireworks and burning effigies on the other. It was a holiday to boot. Soon it became "the most popular state commemoration in the calendar," according to Kevin Doyle's research into the history of the celebrations.

What's more, the combination of All Hallows' (or Saints') Eve (October 31, Halloween) and All Saints' Day (November 1) with Gunpowder Treason Day, November 5, created in effect if not in name another holy week.

So starting on Gunpowder Treason Day in 1606, churches were instructed to use a service involving half a dozen special prayers, including:

> *ALMIGHTY God, . . . We yield thee our unfeigned*
> *thanks and praise for the wonderful and mighty deliv-*
> *erance of our gracious Sovereign King James the First,*

the Queen, the Prince, and all the Royal Branches, with
the Nobility, Clergy and Commons of England, then
assembled in Parliament, by Popish treachery appointed
as sheep to the slaughter, in a most barbarous and savage
manner, beyond the examples of former ages. From this
unnatural Conspiracy, not our merit, but thy mercy; not
our foresight, but thy providence delivered us.

The service was added to the English church's *Book of Common Prayer* in its next edition and remained until removed by royal warrant in 1859, a full two and a half centuries later.

Back in 1606 Parliament also made sure the religious service would have a guaranteed audience. Everyone was required to attend a Church of England morning service on November 5.

From the start, numerous sermons were preached that day, declaring that God indeed had shown His love and favor for England by intervening to save England from the pope, Catholics, and the Devil. God's waiting until the last minute to intervene was His way of showing that He was almighty and on the side of Protestant England.

That was the pious beginning of the day on each Fifth of November. The rest of the day involved bonfires and fireworks, uniquely apt for the nature of the Gunpowder Treason. Fires and fireworks in public places were intended to delight rather than damage, in contrast to the same intended by Catesby, Fawkes, and the other conspirators.

It was also inadvertently providential, indeed essential, for the "guys" we use so familiarly today that the most devastating plot in English history was foiled; it was also providential, and necessary, that the point man, the military expert intending to light the fuses, the first to be arrested and caught in flagrante delicto at midnight November 4, was the one known at first as John Johnson; and that under interrogation, after several days under torture, the stalwart soldier confessed not only the details of the plot but also his real name (Guido or Guy) and those of his co-conspirators.

And it was also providential that so much of the plot was thereby known so soon that the other conspirators were quickly arrested and interrogated or killed while fleeing; that the ringleader Catesby was among those killed, so that his own confession and testimony were not available to focus attention on him rather than Fawkes; that a public trial was promptly conducted, presenting again details of the plot, and recorded for the benefit of posterity as well as the public at that time; and that the conspirators were given yet more publicity by being promptly hanged, drawn, and quartered when the trial was over.

And yet one more providential circumstance, perhaps even more important than all the rest: the celebration of deliverance from the plot by bonfires throughout the kingdom, and the proclamation by Parliament on January 23, 1606, that henceforth every November 5 should repeat the celebration of that deliverance with more bonfires.

Even thought there was no internet, no smartphones, not even a telegraph system to deliver messages quickly, by the end of the day on November 5, 1605, everyone in London and vicinity knew that a terrible plot to blow up the Houses of Parliament had been stopped very early that day, that the man with matches ready to light the fire had been apprehended, and that the king, members of Parliament, and other government officials thus had been spared certain death. It seemed like a miracle, or in any case the hand of providence that had saved the Protestant country.

It helped the celebration that King James himself ordered bells rung and fires to be set throughout the town. On that first Bonfire Day, however, we can be sure that no mention was made of Guy Fawkes, because the prisoner being interrogated was known only as John Johnson.

The Church of England soon became involved, not at first by official decree but by the initiative of enthusiastic priests, emphasizing thanksgiving to God for escaping from destruction. Among the first to preach along those lines was William Barlow, Bishop of Rochester. On Sunday, November 10, just five days after the failed attack, he preached outdoors in the churchyard of St. Paul's to several thousand people.

At one point in a long sermon, the bishop compares the plotters to famous villains in Roman history.

> *Caligula, was but a shadow, for he wished that all the Citizens of Rome, had but one necke, that at one blow hee might cut it off: but this Blood-sucker, not only wished*

it, but contrived it, prepared for it, and was ready to ex-
ecute it. There was but one famous Nero, which for his
crueltie got the name of Nero fro all the rest, him hath
he matched in Affection for when one of Nero his disso-
lute company, had said Me mortuo, when I am deade,
let heaven & earth goe together. Nay said Nero, Me vivo,
while I am alive. So meant Guy Faulkes (the true name
of a false traytor) to have beheld as (hee said) the houses
and bodies flying up; he living & laughing at it. If hee
had solde us for bond-slaves & hand maides, saith Hester
of Haman, yet there had been life, and so hope of returne,
but to make an utter dissolution of the whole State, had
beene a misery incurable was a project most damnable.

Why single out Guy? Because he was the one plotter already caught and implicated for sure. Or perhaps more important, because he was the one who stood by the gunpowder with matches. The name Guy was new enough to the population that Barlow thinks it necessary to follow it with the explanation, "the true name of a false traytor."

6

GUNPOWDER DAYS IN ENGLAND

The Pope and the Guy

The bonfires of November

As the years went on, throughout Britain people celebrated the final part of Gunpowder Treason Day with bonfires, candles, fireworks, bells, music, cheering, and feasting. Kevin Doyle notes,

> *Canterbury accomplished in 1607 what Fawkes had failed to accomplish in 1605: It ignited 106 pounds of gunpowder and 14 pounds of matches, in observation of the day. Later still, in 1610, the officialdom of that city hosted a lavish civic dinner party, in which it then paid*

> *20 shillings for parading, 15 shillings for gunpowder,*
> *14 shillings 7 denari for wine, and 5 shillings for music.*

And in many towns, Doyle adds, "bells joined crackers, cymbals, drums, flutes, salutes, and squibs in creating a cacophony of sorts." By the 1620s, Doyle says, this holiday had become "the most popular state commemoration in the calendar."

Authors of plays and poems took part too. In 1611, Thomas Decker's play "If This Be Not a Good Play, the Devil Is in It" ended up in Hell, with Guy Fawkes there, among others. At one point Fawkes enthusiastically exclaims, "Give fire! Blow all the world up!" Another devil "fires the barrel-tops," whereupon Fawkes says, "I shall be grinded into dust. It falls! I am mad!" And a little later, Fawkes exults:

> *So, all the billets lie close. Glorious bonfire! Pontifical*
> *bonfire! Brave heads to contrive this, gallant souls to*
> *conspire in't, resolute hand to seal this with my blood,*
> *through fire through flint. Ha, ha, ha! Whither fly myself*
> *to Heaven, friends to honour, none to the halter, enemies*
> *to massacre. Ha, ha! Dismal tragical-comedy now?*

In 1614, in "Bartholomew Fair: A Comedy," Ben Jonson had the chapman puppeteer Lanthorn Leatherhead say:

> *O the Motions, that I Lanthorn Leatherhead have given*
> *light to, i' my time, since my Master Pod died! Jerusalem*

> *was a stately thing; and so was Ninive, and the City of*
> *Norwich, and Sodom and Gomorrah; with the rising o'*
> *the Prentises, and pulling down the Bawdy Houses there*
> *upon Shrove-Tues-day; but the Gunpowder-plot, there*
> *was a get-penny! I have presented that to an eighteen or*
> *twenty Pence Audience, nine times in an Afternoon. Your*
> *home-born Projects prove ever the best, they are so easie*
> *and familiar; they put too much Learning i' their things*
> *now o'days.*

In 1626, young John Milton, while at Cambridge University at the ripe age of 17, penned 226 lines in Latin for a poem about Gunpowder Treason titled "In quintum Novembris." It's in an obscure poetic style known as Alexandrian epyllion. In accord with the style and the Latin, the names of all the characters are from classical mythology, but there is no mistaking the allusion to Guy's role (in translation):

> *I command you to hasten there on swift feet, and let them be*
> *blown into thin air by Hellish powder, both the King and*
> *his Lords, and also his wicked offspring; and as many men*
> *as have been burning with zeal for the true Faith you must*
> *make partners in your plan and the agents of our work.*

An illustrated poem by one Francis Herring, published in London in 1641, begins with a mention of the incendiary point man:

See, here, the Popish Pouder-plots fair thriving,
Fauks and his Father-Satan sit contriving
The fatal-Instruments, to puffe and blow
Hell out of Earth, a State to over-throw,
At Once, for All. . . .
Faukes has now become no less than the son of the devil.

Among other ways of remembering November 5, in the 1620s some church parishes began observing it as a day for charity, collecting funds to support hospitals, education, even clothing for the poor.

At this early stage, the name Guy isn't a magic word. The day is called Gunpowder Treason Day, or Gunpowder Night, or just Bonfire Night, focusing on Catholics and the pope instead of Guy Fawkes alone. When the commemoration was sermons and church bells, Fawkes did not figure prominently. He was a strong, staunch, and courageous Catholic, but not any kind of theologian, preacher, or prophet, and not the mastermind of the plot. Unlike the pope and other high officials, Fawkes was known not for his rank or position but only for his acts on the night of the original Gunpowder Day.

But thanks to the bonfires and fireworks, reflecting benevolently what Fawkes had intended malevolently, Guy was far from forgotten. A gradual change in focus began in the 1630s, thanks to the bonfires.

Bonfires had been features of English celebrations long before 1605, so they fit perfectly with the new holiday of November

5. And that began to turn attention to Guy—"the Guy," that is, beginning the transformation from terrorist to stuffed effigy, a transformation crucial to the term we use nowadays.

Even at bonfires, though, it took a little while for Guy, or rather his likeness, to make an appearance. For example, in Norwich, Doyle notes that "up to 1625, that town burned in its bonfire not only debris and wood but also a host of models or relics of popery, including an altarstone, a crucifix, a habit, a lectionary, a pax, and a surplice." No Guy yet.

During the English civil war of 1642–1651, both sides viewed the November 5 celebration as their own, so even with regime change it continued without interruption. In 1647, as the civil war was coming to an end with King Charles in prison, Londoners were treated to a spectacular series of fireworks, courtesy of a gunner named George Browne, including

> Faux with his darke Lanthorne, and many fire-boxes, lights, and lamps, ushering the Pope into England, intimating the full Plot to destroy Englands King and Parliament.

Again, though, the last name Faux rather than Guy was used to refer to the devilish traitor. Guy by itself was still more often the name or title of many a French hero. But then came the practice of making a combustible caricature effigy of Guy Fawkes and parading it through the streets before being tossed on the

Gunpowder Treason Day bonfire along with "the guy"s companion "the pope."

Another reason for thanksgiving on November 5 came in 1688. That was when the Protestant Prince of Orange, William III, landed on the coast of England with a fleet of ships and a large army. He soon swept away the forces of King James II, and, with his wife Mary, James's Protestant daughter, William and Mary became joint monarchs.

James II had given Catholics relief because of his religious tolerance, which he needed since he was a convert to Catholicism himself. With James's newborn son, also a Catholic, as heir apparent, Protestants in England felt even more threatened. With the "glorious revolution" of 1688 bringing William and Mary to the throne instead, England remained safely Protestant. The English saw it as one more sign of God's favor.

With the experience of that narrow escape in mind, during the rest of the 17th century and the beginning of the 18th, the anti-Catholic sermons maintained and even increased their vitriol, and life became even harder for recusant English Catholics, no matter how loyal to William and Mary. If the Gunpowder Plot had almost succeeded in wiping out the Church of England by destroying the whole government, people worried, what extreme might the next Catholic attack intend?

As it finally turned out, nothing so extreme happened, though Catholic plots of various sorts continued from time to time. In the 18th century, for example, England was threatened by the Old

Pretender, son of Charles II, and then the Young Pretender, son of the Old, known as Bonnie Prince Charlie, both Catholics and supported by France. Losing one-sided battles in 1715 and then in 1746, they never got close to restoring Catholic Stuart rule in England, but they kept the country worried.

Never in the following centuries was there anything nearly as dreadful as Gunpowder Treason. With the benefit of hindsight we know this. But for two centuries after 1605 religion in England still was in a grim, divisive situation, an English system planted atop a native Catholic one. Not until the 19th century would the two Christian faiths of England be peaceably reconciled.

During the 18th century, celebrations of Guy Fawkes Night continued as vigorously as ever, if not more so. Local celebrations were marked by begging, fights, food, fireworks, and bonfires that over the years seemed to become more spectacular the more distant they were from the original Fifth of November.

As the centuries went on, the original plotters became more distant in time and memory. Effigies prepared for bonfires often were contemporary villains rather than the original arch-enemies—except for the guy. Maybe that was because Guy Fawkes was the only one always associated only with Gunpowder Treason. He was no longer a living threat, just an arch-villain safely dead long ago, not so much to fear as to laugh at and an excuse for children to beg "pennies for the Guy," supposedly to finance the effigy of Guy Fawkes destined for the flames.

By the 19th century, Catholics were no longer a threat in England, so the pope wasn't always an appropriate target. But Guy

Fawkes was, safely frozen in history as someone who had been ready to perpetrate the greatest evil back in 1605. It became necessary to remind each other why Bonfire Night, or Guy Fawkes Night, should arouse anything but merriment.

Merriment, rather than fear, is exemplified by a poem well known nowadays. It's considered a folk poem, apparently composed in the 18th century, but not widely published until the 19th. Nowadays it's often used to give the reason for November 5 celebrations. Its happy fearlessness is indicated by being sometimes described as a poem for infants and children. There are many variants, but they all agree on the first stanza, with minor variations in wording.

Remember, remember
The fifth of November,
Gunpowder treason and plot;
I see no reason
Why Gunpowder treason
Should ever be forgot!

Guy Fawkes and his companions
Did the scheme contrive,
To blow the King and Parliament
All up alive.

Threescore barrels, laid below,
To prove old England's overthrow.
But, by God's providence, him they catch,
With a dark lantern, lighting a match!

 A stick and a stake
 For King James's sake!
 If you won't give me one,
 I'll take two,
 The better for me,
 And the worse for you.

The next stanza, and others along those lines, since the 19th century have often been omitted, since Catholicism and the Church of England were finally reconciled.

 A rope, a rope, to hang the Pope,
 A penn'orth of cheese to choke him,
 A pint of beer to wash it down,
 And a jolly good fire to burn him.
 Holloa, boys! holloa, boys! make the bells ring!
 Holloa, boys! holloa boys! God save the King!
 Hip, hip, hooor-r-r-ray!

And so it has continued, down to the present day in England and the United Kingdom, though with less politics and more merriment. Guy Fawkes Day has become more like the present-day American Halloween, and indeed Halloween is becoming more prevalent and popular even in England, on the way perhaps to eclipsing November 5 altogether.

7

POPE NIGHT IN AMERICA

New World Guy

The American Revolution throws cold water on the Guy

As the English began to establish colonies in North America, their settlers as a matter of course brought the most prominent and celebrated English holiday with them. And as long as the colonies remained English, Gunpowder Treason Day continued to be celebrated with increasing enthusiasm throughout most of the colonies, both the sermons in the mornings and the bonfires at night.

The most notable celebrations of the day were in Massachusetts, but all the colonies participated in various ways. Though the Puritan government of Massachusetts was not always sympathetic to making it a special day of thanksgiving, let alone a day to be idle from work, the bonfire builders and mischief makers kept busy from the start.

In 1607, less than two years after Gunpowder Night, the first English-speaking American colony was established in what is now Virginia. With a charter from King James I, and the name Jamestown, it maintained good relations with the king and thus very likely celebrated Gunpowder Night, at least the bonfires. But disease, chronic shortages of food, and war with Indians beset the colony throughout its early years, and their chronicles and reports make almost no mention of Gunpowder Night, very likely because at starvation level they wouldn't have had time or strength for such a celebration.

Because Jamestown remained affiliated with the Church of England, however, that colony would have observed the church calendar designating November 5 a day of thanksgiving. The memory of November 5, 1605, was vivid enough that members of the Jamestown colony in 1607 had to swear an oath not to attempt anything like what Guy Fawkes and the other conspirators had undertaken. You can almost smell the gunpowder:

> I. . . . . . M. . . . . . *doe trulie and sincerely acknowl-*
> *edge. professe testifie and declare in my Conscience before*
> *God & the world, That our Soveraigne Lord King James*
> *ys lawfull and rightful King of Great Britaine and of*
> *the Colony of Virginia, and of all other his Majesties*
> *Dominions and Countries. And that ye pope neither of*
> *himselfe, nor by any Authoretie of the Church or See of*

Rome, or by any other meanes (with any other) hath any
power or authoritie to depose the King or to dispose any
of his Majesties Dominions.

Meanwhile, to the north, the first recorded observance of Gunpowder Night in America happened in the Plymouth colony of New England in 1623, just three years after the Pilgrims arrived there. There was a little trouble with the bonfire, as Governor William Bradford wrote:

This fire was occasioned by some of the seamen that were
roistering in a house where it first began, making a great
fire in cold weather, which broke out of the chimney into
the thatch. . . .

The house in which it began was right against their
storehouse, which they had much ado to save, in which were
their common store and all their provisions, the which, if
they had been lost, the plantation had been overthrown.
But through God's mercy it was saved by the great dil-
igence of the people and care of the [government]. . . .

But a trusty company . . . suspected some malicious
dealing, if not plain treachery, and whether it was only
suspicion or not, God knows; but this is certain, that when
the tumult was greatest, there was a voice heard (but from
whom it was not known) that bid them look about them,
for all were not friends that were near them. . . . But God
kept them from this danger, whatever was intended,

That was not only the first but apparently the only Massachusetts religious celebration of the Fifth of November for some time. The Church of England's calendar of feasts wasn't followed in the Massachusetts colony, but nobody in authority, governors or clergy, dared to advocate abolishing the November 5 celebration.

Further to the north, the Newfoundland colony weighed in on Gunpowder Treason in 1628 with a book of epigrams and verses by Governor Robert Hayman. His poem, "Of the Gunpowder Holly-day, the 5. of November," includes this stanza:

> *The Powder-Traytors, Guy Vaux, and his mates,*
> *Who by a Hellish plot sought Saints estates,*
> *Have in our Kalendar unto their shame,*
> *A joyfull Holy-day cald by their Name.*

By the 18th century, both the preaching and the bonfires of Gunpowder Day reached a peak of participation and enthusiasm. But then came the American Revolution.

The Revolution inadvertently encouraged a rethinking of the role of Guy Fawkes. The guy was still tossed in the bonfire of Guy Fawkes Night, but American colonists found themselves with the same goal as Fawkes: removing the English monarchy and government.

Ironically, by the mid-18th century, New England commemorations of Gunpowder Treason were at their height. Guy Fawkes wasn't as prominent a figure in New England as he was in Old England, however. Because of strong anti-Catholic sentiment in pious New England, the focus there was more on the pope—and the Devil, and other current personages, including Stuart pretenders to the English throne in the 18th century. In contrast, Guy Fawkes and his fellow conspirators of 1605 were less emphasized as the years went on, becoming historical figures from the past and not a present danger.

Each New England locality developed its own way of celebrating Gunpowder Night, but all involved something like this: men and boys would construct effigies of the hated figures. Boys would go house to house with the figures, demanding cash contributions for the expense of building them. At night, the effigies would be burned in great bonfires.

Leading all others in celebrating was Boston. By mid-18th century the Boston bonfire of every November 5 ended up with an extra act: a brawl between North Enders and South Enders armed with stones and barrel staves. The gangs of the North End were pro-royalty, those of the South End anti-royalty, but their chief interest on November 5 was to drink, fight each other, and capture the other's effigy of the pope. Both papal effigies ended up in a bonfire outside the gates of the city. The bonfire remained decidedly anti-Catholic.

A lengthy broadside poem sold by Boston printers' boys for Gunpowder Night 1768 starts like this:

1. HUZZA! brave Boys, behold the Pope,
Pretender and Old-Nick,
How they together lay their Heads,
To plot a poison Trick?

2. To blow up KING and PARLIAMENT
To Flitters, rent and torn:
—Oh! blund'ring Poet, Since the Plot,
Was this Pretender born. . . .

4. Come on, brave Youths, drag on your Pope
Let's see his frightful Phiz:
Let's view his Features rough and fierce,
That Map of Ugliness!

5. Distorted Joints, so huge and broad!
So horribly drest up!
'Twould puzzle Newton's Self to tell,
The D——l from the Pope.

And so on, for a total of 28 stanzas mocking the Pope, with no mention of Guy Fawkes.

That also was about to undergo a change after 1776. General Washington, in particular, wanted no part of anti-Catholicism. Among other reasons, he was hoping to persuade French-Canadian Catholics to join in the Revolution. In 1775, camped near Boston, he was displeased with the bloody Boston fights. He issued this Order in Quarters to his army on November 5:

> As the Commander in Chief has been apprized of a design
> form'd for the observance of that ridiculous and childish
> custom of burning the Effigy of the pope, He cannot help
> expressing his surprise that there should be Officers and
> Soldiers in this army so void of common sense, as not to

see the impropriety of such a step at this Juncture; at a
Time when we are solliciting, and have really obtain'd,
the friendship and alliance of the people of Canada,
whom we ought to consider as Brethren embarked in the
same Cause. The defence of the general Liberty of America:

At such a juncture, and in such Circumstances, to
be insulting their Religion, is so monstrous, as not to be
suffered or excused; indeed instead of offering the most re-
mote insult, it is our duty to address public thanks to these
our Brethren, as to them we are so much indebted for every
late happy Success over the common Enemy in Canada.

Boston went ahead and celebrated November 5 anyhow that year, but Washington's declaration remained and helped tone down the anti-Catholic rhetoric. So Washington did his part in downplaying Guy Fawkes Day by directly attacking the religious premise for Pope Night celebrations.

At about the same time, John Adams inadvertently added to the downplaying of Pope Night by ignoring it. He foresaw instead an entirely different American occasion for celebratory bonfires. In a letter to his wife Abigail, he was off by just two days in his prediction:

3 July 1776

The Second Day of July 1776, will be the most
memorable Epocha, in the History of America. I am
apt to believe that it will be celebrated, by succeeding
Generations, as the great anniversary Festival. It ought

> *to be commemorated, as the Day of Deliverance by*
> *solemn Acts of Devotion to God Almighty. It ought to be*
> *solemnized with Pomp and Parade, with Shews, Games,*
> *Sports, Guns, Bells, Bonfires and Illuminations from one*
> *End of this Continent to the other from this Time forward*
> *forever more.*

And so when in due course the United States adopted a Constitution and added a Bill of Rights, the first clause of the first amendment declared:

> *Congress shall make no law respecting an establishment*
> *of religion, or prohibiting the free exercise thereof.*

This did not immediately quash all celebrations of November 5, but they gradually diminished until by mid-19th century few remained. And that was necessary in order to pave the way for a very different use of "guy."

8

MY PRONOUN, 'TIS OF THEE

Thou Art Lost and Gone Forever

Help wanted: pronoun

We need to step aside for a moment from the march of English and American history to observe a rare development that allowed "guys" not just to survive but to establish itself in the heart of the English language. That development culminated in the 18th century just as "guy" was beginning to flex its muscles and broaden its range of meanings. What was it? It was the loss of an essential element of the language we use every day: the personal pronoun "thou."

Whether or not we study the grammar of English, the personal pronouns don't care. We use them all the time in any case. As the name "pronoun" implies, they take the place of nouns, and of phrases centered on nouns, so that we don't have to endlessly repeat those nouns.

If there were no pronouns, Abraham Lincoln wouldn't have been able to say at Gettysburg:

> *The world will little note, nor long remember what we say here, but it can never forget what they did here. It is for us the living, rather, to be dedicated here to the unfinished work which they who fought here have thus far so nobly advanced.*

Instead, using only pronoun-free language, he would have had to say something like this:

> *The world will little note, nor long remember what the living persons at this ceremony say here, but it can never forget what those who gave their lives on this battlefield did here. It is for the living persons at this ceremony, rather, to be dedicated here to the unfinished work which the persons who fought here have thus far so nobly advanced.*

Occasionally people deliberately choose to refer to themselves by name rather than by pronoun, as Richard Nixon did in 1962 after losing the election for governor of California:

> *You don't have Nixon to kick around anymore because, gentlemen, this is my last press conference.*

But even that statement still has two pronouns, "you" and "my." In a truly pronoun-free environment, the future president would have had to say:

> *The media don't have Nixon to kick around anymore be-*
> *cause, gentlemen, this is Richard M. Nixon's last press*
> *conference.*

So what happened that allowed "guys" or "you guys" to be a personal pronoun, and an essential one too? It was a once-in-a-millennium moment that was improbably available at just the right time. One pronoun dropped out, to be replaced by another, which in turn made way for "guys" big time.

The dropout was "thou." Its loss is lamented—inadvertently—in the chorus of a familiar 19th-century song:

> *O my darling,*
> *O my darling,*
> *O my darling Clementine,*
> *Thou art lost and gone forever,*
> *Dreadful sorry, Clementine.*

It's a dreadful tale, though it sometimes seems to be tongue in cheek. It is a well-known song of California gold rush times, a purportedly sad folk ballad that draws laughs for its inept diction, clumsy rhymes, and trifling sentiments ("her shoes were number nine," "herring boxes without topses," "then I kissed her little sister and forgot my Clementine").

It was written around 1864 and published in 1885. And over the years since, not only Clementine was lost but "thou art." Modern versions generally substitute "you are," because "thou" continues to grow ever more obsolete.

A pronoun is so fundamental to a language that it rarely gets lost. And even more rarely does it get lost without a replacement, as "thou" did.

Personal pronouns come in different forms for different grammatical uses. "Thou" is used as the subject of a sentence, as in "Clementine," along with its derivatives "thee," as in "I give thee my word," and the possessives "thy" and "thine," as in "Go wash thy face and thine ears." They are all different forms of the now obsolete second-person singular pronoun.

English Personal Pronouns: Old English (1000 years ago) (modern spellings used for all periods)	
Singular	Plural
Singular—1st person I, me, mine	Plural—1st person we, our, ours
Singular—2nd person thou, thee, thine	Plural—2nd person you, your, yours
Singular—3rd person he, him, his she, her, hers it, its	Plural—3rd person they, them, theirs

English Personal Pronouns: Middle English
(500 years ago)
(modern spellings used for all periods)

Singular	Plural
Singular—1st person	Plural—1st person
I, me, mine	we, our, ours
Singular—2nd person	Plural—2nd person
thou, thee, thine	you, your, yours
you, your, yours	
Singular—3rd person	Plural—3rd person
he, him, his	they, them, theirs
she, her, hers	
it, its	

English Personal Pronouns: 18th Century
(modern spellings used for all periods)

Singular	Plural
Singular—1st person	Plural—1st person
I, me, mine	we, our, ours
Singular—2nd person	Plural – 2nd person
you, your, yours	you, your, yours
Singular—3rd person	Plural—3rd person
he, him, his	they, them, theirs
she, her, hers	
it, its	

English Personal Pronouns: Today
(21st Century)
(modern spellings used for all periods)

Singular	Plural
Singular—1st person I, me, mine	Plural—1st person we, our, ours
Singular—2nd person **you, your, yours** y'all	Plural—2nd person **guys, you guys, your guys',** **you guys';** y'all, all y'all, etc.
Singular—3rd person he, him, his she, her, hers it, its	Plural—3rd person they, them, theirs

Losing pronouns seems careless. Pronouns are not like nouns and verbs, adjectives and adverbs, which our language is full of (half a million or more of them). But we have just a handful of pronouns, and they have the important job of connecting what we say to the people and things in the world around us: *We* like *it, They* admire *her, I* enjoy *him*, and so on.

They are called personal pronouns, because they refer to people. Or persons, if you will. We refer to ourselves with first-person pronouns: *I, me, my, mine*, in the singular (just one of us); *we, us, our, ours* in the plural (more than one). Those are called first person because they refer to the first person in anything we say or write; not necessarily the leader or most powerful person, just the one who is doing the speaking or writing .

Third-person pronouns refer to others who aren't directly involved in the conversation: *he, she, it, his, her, hers, its,* in the singular (just one); *they, them, their, theirs*, in the plural (more than one).

And then there is our particular concern, the second-person pronouns. That's someone I'm speaking to or directly addressing in writing. With "thou" disappearing, "you" stretched from the plural to cover the singular too, with forms *you, your, yours*. The only problem is, under that arrangement you can't tell singular from plural, which personal pronouns need to do.

As long as "thou" was available, English had no such problem. In Old English times, a thousand years ago, English had the ancestors of "thou" and "you" for second-person singular pronouns. "Art thou Beowulf?" they could ask, and "Where are ye from?" Simple and uncomplicated enough.

In what we call the Middle English period, from about 1100 to 1500 C.E., the English language added a complication that would eventually lead to the 18th-century disappearance of "thou." In common with other major European languages, including French, Italian, and Spanish, English speakers began addressing their superiors and even their equals as "you," rather than "thou," or some other plural pronoun, even when they were speaking to only one person. In English, "thou" did continue for centuries to be used when talking with servants and others of lower class, as well as in intimate relations like those of families or lovers.

Take, for example, the modern compliment (or attempt at compliment) addressed to one person:

You are very beautiful.

Now, still speaking to that one person, make it singular or plural, depending on who we're speaking to:

Thou art very beautiful. (speaking to a servant)
You are very beautiful (speaking to the Queen at a reception)

We find the new choice for second-person singular, for example, in the medieval Arthurian romance *Sir Gawain and the Green Knight*, written just before 1400. In the opening scene, King Arthur and his knights and ladies are enjoying their Christmas feast when a strange man on horseback gallops right into the hall, wielding an axe, his horse and axe and himself entirely green. The knights and ladies stare in silent amazement. After a long silence Arthur speaks up:

> *Alight down and stay, I pray thee,*
> *And whatever thy will is, we shall know later.*

Arthur as king is highest ranking in the room and would address everyone there as "thou." Instead of showing deference to Arthur's status, however, the green knight replies,

> *But for the fame of thee, sir, is lifted up so high,*
> *And thy town and thy knights are the best . . .*

And so it goes for the rest of the story, Gawain and the green knight "thou"ing each other, while the court always addresses the king respectfully with "you."

That is just one of many Middle English examples. The older use of singular pronouns continued in the English Renaissance, and of course it shows up in Shakespeare.

In the first scene of *Julius Caesar*, for example, we find the tribune Marullus talking with commoners. Marullus begins with "you," but when he recognizes the lower rank of the person he addresses, he quickly switches to "thou." The commoner, of course, still respectfully says "you" in reply.

MARULLUS. You, sir, what trade are you?

SECOND COMMONER. Truly, sir, in respect of a fine workman, I am but, as you would say, a cobbler.

MARULLUS. But what trade art thou? Answer me directly.

SECOND COMMONER. A trade, sir, that, I hope, I may use with a safe conscience; which is, indeed, sir, a mender of bad soles.

MARULLUS. What trade, thou knave? Thou naughty knave, what trade?

SECOND COMMONER. Nay, I beseech you, sir, be not out with me: yet, if you be out, sir, I can mend you.

MARULLUS. What meanest thou by that? Mend me, thou saucy fellow!

Likewise in *Richard III*, we find clueless Lord Hastings respectfully addressed as "you" by the Duke of Buckingham, who uses "thou" in an aside to let the audience know what he really thinks.

HASTINGS. 'Tis like enough for I stay dinner there.

BUCKINGHAM (ASIDE). And supper too, although thou know'st it not. (ALOUD) Come, will you go?

Legal documents from that time also show that people were putting *thee* and *thou* to use as insults. The attorney general at Sir Walter Raleigh's trial taunted Raleigh by saying "All that he did was at thy instigation, thou viper; for I thou thee, thou traitor."

But by his time "thou" was fading. Why it did nobody knows for sure, but there is no question that already even in the 16th century more and more people avoided "thou."

In other European languages, the plain forms of address equivalent to "thou" remain to this day, along with the polite plural alternatives equivalent to "you" or "they." In English, the polite form totally vanquished the plain one, except in archaic remnants. Perhaps there was more of a democratic spirit among English speakers, thinking everyone deserves respect, even the lowliest of servants. Perhaps more likely, it was by no means easy to determine at once whether a stranger you met was of equal or higher or lower status. The safest choice, in that case, would be "you." That would always imply respect, rather than "thou," which could well have been an insult.

In any case, as "thou" receded, it rapidly became more and more of an insult to use "thou" instead of "you," because now instead of routinely saying "thou" to someone of lower class, there was always the polite alternative "you."

As the change was spreading rapidly in the 17th century, the new religious sect known as the Quakers were moving in the opposite direction. Pointedly avoiding the polite "you" as too deferential, they insisted on the use of plain "thou" for all occasions, considering all people equal and not to be deferred to. They eliminated "thou," though, using "thee" alone. At about the same time, in the rest of the English language, "ye" was vanishing and "you" took its place in Quaker talk.

George Fox, founder of the Quakers, once said, "We were often beset and abused, and sometimes in danger of our lives for using these words to some proud men, who would say, 'What! You ill-bred clown, do you thou me?'"

As that statement indicates, the Quakers were far from admired for their insistence on "thou." It may be that reaction to the Quakers led to the final demise of "thou" from present-day discourse.

This doesn't mean "thou" was completely gone. "Thou" persisted in religious tradition that was loath to change familiar words. The King James Bible of the early 17th century followed the pronoun conventions of its predecessor, the Tyndale version, maintaining the older, simpler Old English distinction of "thou" addressing one person or divine figure, "you" for many. And since the King James Bible is so admired for its language, it has helped keep "thou" in print even to the present day.

Another American exception is patriotic songs, at least those written in the United States in the 19th century, like Samuel Francis Smith's 1831 "America," which begins:

My country, 'tis of thee,
Sweet land of liberty,

Of thee I sing;
Land where my fathers died,
Land of the pilgrims' pride,
From ev'ry mountainside
Let freedom ring!

My native country, thee,
Land of the noble free,
Thy name I love;
I love thy rocks and rills,
Thy woods and templed hills;
My heart with rapture thrills,
Like that above.

Likewise in "America the Beautiful," written in 1893 by Katherine Lee Bates, inspired by a view of Pikes Peak:

O beautiful for spacious skies,
For amber waves of grain,
For purple mountain majesties
Above the fruited plain!
America! America!
God shed His grace on thee,
And crown thy good with brotherhood
From sea to shining sea!

O beautiful for pilgrim feet
Whose stern impassioned stress

A thoroughfare for freedom beat
Across the wilderness.
America! America!
God mend thine ev'ry flaw,
Confirm thy soul in self-control,
Thy liberty in law.

Other songs, however, don't attempt old-fashioned "thou"s. "The Star-Spangled Banner" (1814), for example, begins "O say, can 'you' see."

All this is to explain a very unusual situation: how it became possible for "guy," referring at first to a certain kind of man, then to any kind of man, and eventually even to include women, to become our present-day second-person plural pronoun. The space was vacant, and no word or phrase was successful at filling it in the 18th century or indeed the 19th. So the space remained open until "you guys" came along in the 20th century.

9

GUYS IN RAGS

Raised to respectability

As early as the 17th century, the effigy burned at November 5 bonfires came to be known as "the Guy." That easily became "the guy," since there was no difference at all in pronunciation—and only in more modern times were capital letters restricted to proper names.

Furthermore, the fact that Fawkes was but one Guy among many, as we have noted in Chapter 3, made the transition easy. The other Guys generally had better reputations. They were well known for feats of daring and courage, above all the legendary homegrown Englishman Guy of Warwick. In the histories and chronicles we also read, for example, of Guy de Beauchamp, tenth Earl of Warwick, and Guy of Lusignan, Crusader king of Jerusalem, who lost that kingdom to Saladin.

And the fact that these Guys were human made it easy to make the transition from arch-villain to effigy and then back again to human being.

The extensive use of their names also led to the appearance of forms of "guy" that prefigure later uses, such as "a guy" in this 1640 collection of poems by Thomas Carew:

> *we have a guy, a beavis, or some true round-table night as*
> *ever fought for lady, to each beauty brought.*

In 1659, William Prynne writes of "a guy faux with his dark Lanthorn to blow up a parliament."

A 1655 poem "Truth's integrity" has this line, "brave guy earl of warwick, that champion so stout: with his warlike behavior, through the world he did stray to win his phillis favour."

Thomas Merton's 1658 play "Love and War: A Tragedy" puts a character on stage with two swords and armor, saying, "my helmet Shews a force to kill a guy, or Hercules."

From 1676, *The Baronage of England* by Sir William Dugdale: "this guy being then dead without issue."

Richard Johnson's 1696 history of the seven champions of Christendom uses a possessive form: "it was sir guys fortune to met with the Egyptian king."

That's how language change often occurs. A word or phrase used in one context becomes convenient to use in another, often without the user being aware of making the change. And that's because every human has to learn a language from scratch, rather than inheriting it. In the process of listening and then interpreting what others say, we now and then come up with different interpretations.

The examples above look like modern uses of "guy": "a guy," "this guy," "brave guy," "the same guy." In larger contexts, they aren't always modern. Here is Carew's fuller context for "a guy":

> *we bring prince arthur, or the brave st: george himselfe*
> *(great Queene) to you, you'll soone discerne him; and we*
> *have a guy, a beavis, or some true round-table knight, as*
> *everfought for lady, to each beauty brought.*

Surrounded by the noblest of chivalry—Prince Arthur, St. George, and "a beavis" (Sir Bevis of Hampton), the arch-villain Guy Fawkes would be way out of place. Instead, Carew must have meant "a Guy" like Guy of Warwick or Guy of Lusignan. Because there was more than one prominent Guy, "a guy" was possible here. So it was already a familiar phrase, ready to take on the meaning of "an effigy of Guy Fawkes" and then "a male human of the lowest order," and then (all of this is gradual, taking centuries) "any male," as it is today.

Even more modern-sounding is *The Antiquities of Warwickshire* by Sir William Dugdale (1656). Since it tells about quite a few Guys, it has many phrases that would seem perfectly modern today: which guy, this guy, the famous guy (yes, of Warwick), the warlike guy, the renowned guy, the sometime famous guy, our noble guy, the same guy, the valiant guy, the said guy, the said great guy. Many of these phrases, like "the famous guy," appear again and again in *The Antiquities*.

Thanks to the custom that developed of youths begging "pennies for the guy" to help finance November 5 bonfires, it was easy enough for the meaning of "guy" to develop a plural "guys," extending the word beyond the name of the point man for the Gunpowder Plot. At times all of the effigies to be burned were referred to as "guys."

That, in turn, led to the extended meaning of "guy" as a real flesh-and-blood man, though at first, because of Fawkes's notoriety, the effigy was a particularly disreputable or garishly garbed one.

As the *Oxford English Dictionary* notes, this "guy," in bonfires built for November 5, "is habited in grotesquely ragged and ill-assorted garments." Its earliest example is from 1806, in a letter from W. Burrell to C. K. Sharpe: "A month ago there was neither shape nor make in me. . . . No guy ever matched me." And in 1825 W. Hone wrote in his *Every-day Book*: "Formerly an old cocked hat was the reigning fashion for a 'Guy.' "

Around the start of the 19th century, then, "guys" were still the feature of Gunpowder Treason bonfires. But as the years went on, their connection to the specific character of Guy Fawkes diminished, especially in the United States. That helped the generic "guy" gradually lose its ill repute and begin to be used as a slang term to designate any man, at least in conversation among men who were uncouth or pretentious.

Americans took the lead in this development. They found it difficult to focus on Fawkes as the arch-traitor, considering that they too had aimed to overthrow the British government. It was also hard for Americans to get excited about a man across the ocean, two centuries earlier, who was trying to do more or less what Americans had been doing in the Revolutionary War. Maybe he wasn't such a villain.

And since in the meantime English had lost its second-person plural pronoun, "you" having to serve both as singular and plural, "guys" or "you guys" became a candidate for the unambiguous plural. But that happened later.

Along with singular "guy" came plural "guys." That was even further removed from Guy Fawkes, who remained a singular guy, not plural. Since both "guy" and "guys" were informal and lower-class slang, both very likely had been used for decades before the earliest known instances. In any case, around the time of the American Civil War, "guy" and "guys" begin to appear in print.

For example, Theodore Winthrop's 1862 novel about New York during the Revolutionary War has both singular and plural:

> *Peter's seedy coat was freshness and elegance compared to the scarecrow uniforms it now encountered. Our Revolutionary officers were braves at heart, but mostly* **Guys** *in costume.*
>
> *And you, O Peter Skerrett! you have shaved off your moustache and donned a coat much too small—you have made a* **guy** *of yourself for your first interview with this angel! Shall the personal impression she may already have made be here revised and corrected?*

In 1863, Winthrop's posthumous collection *Life in the Open Air, and Other Papers* used "guys" to describe horses in a chapter on "Washington as a Camp" during the Civil War. Winthrop was one of the first casualties of the war.

> *Here, by the way, let me pause to ask, as a horseman, though a foot-soldier, why generals and other gorgeous fellows make such* **guys** *of their horses with trappings. If the horse is a screw, cover him thick with saddlecloths, girths, cruppers, breast-bands, and as much brass and tinsel as your pay will enable you to buy; but if not a screw, let his fair proportions be seen as much as may be, and don't bother a lover of good horse-flesh to eliminate so much uniform before he can see what is beneath.*

Also in 1863, we find incompetent travel writers derided as "guys" in Gail Hamilton's (Mary Abigail Dodge) *Gala-Days*. In a dialogue, she tells her brother Halicarnassus:

> *"I travel to write. I do not write because I have travelled. I am not going to subordinate my book to my adventures. My adventures are going to be arranged beforehand with a view to my book."*
>
> *Halicarnassus. "A most original way of getting up a book!"*
>
> *Hamilton. "Not in the least. It is the most common thing in the world. Look at our dear British cousins."*

> Halicarnassus. "And see them make **guys** of them-
> selves. They visit a magnificent country that is trying the
> experiment of the world, and write about their shaving-
> soap and their babies' nurses."

Louisa May Alcott has a "guy," an overdressed girl, in her 1868 "Kitty's Class Day and Other Stories":

> As she stepped out of the cars at Cambridge, Jack opened his
> honest blue eyes and indulged in a low whistle of astonish-
> ment: for if there was anything he especially hated, it was
> the trains, chignons and tiny bonnets then in fashion. He
> was very fond of Kitty, and prided himself on being able to
> show his friends a girl who was charming, and yet not over-
> dressed. "She has made a regular **guy** of herself; I won't
> tell her so, and the dear little soul shall have a jolly time in
> spite of her fuss and feathers. But I do wish she had let her
> hair alone and worn that pretty hat of hers."

And we find a "guy" meditating to himself in Anna Dickinson's "What Answer?" published in 1868:

> No, that will never do! Go to her looking like such a
> **guy**? Nary time. I'll get scrubbed, and put on a clean
> shirt, and make myself decent, before she sees me. She al-
> ways used to look nice as a new pin, and she liked me to

look so too; so I'd better put my best foot foremost when she hasn't laid eyes on me for such an age. I'm fright enough, anyway, goodness knows, with my thinness, and my old lame leg.

The noted author Frances Anne Kemble wrote "Old Woman's Gossip, VIII," for the March 1876 issue of the *Atlantic Monthly*:

*To me, of course, my first fancy ball was an event of unmixed delight, especially as my mother had provided for me a lovely Anne Boleyn costume of white satin, point-lace, and white Roman pearls, which raised my satisfaction to rapture. The two Harrys, however, far from partaking of my ecstasy, protested, pouted, begged off, all but broke into open rebellion at the idea of making what they called "***guys***" and "chimney-sweeps"' of themselves; and though the painful sense of any singularity might have been mitigated by the very numerous company of their fellow-fools assembled in the ball-room, to keep them in countenance, and the very unpretending costume of simple and elegant black velvet in which my mother had attired them, as Hamlet and Laertes (it must have been in their very earliest college days), they hid themselves behind the ball-room door and never showed as much as their noses or their toes.*

Bret Harte, in *Drift from Two Shores* (1878), has a girl observing "guys" wearing "bedrabbled" clothes:

> As they plodded wearily toward her, she bit her red lips, smacked them on her cruel little white teeth like a festive and sprightly ghoul, and lisped: —"You do look so like **guys**! For all the world like those English shopkeepers we met on the Righi, doing the three-guinea excursion in their Sunday clothes!" Certainly the spectacle of these exotically plumed bipeds, whose fine feathers were already bedrabbled by sand and growing limp in the sea breeze, was somewhat dissonant with the rudeness of sea and sky and shore.

Characters in Augustin Daly's comedy *Love in Tandem* (1879) likewise use "guys" to mean garish attire:

Dick. In every well-regulated family everything should be in harmony!

Aprilla. Harmony! Music the soul of harmony! and that ridiculous fencing! Two men dressed like **guys**. Why, you have only to look at the teachers to see the difference.

Dick. Indeed!

Aprilla. Madame Laurette is a lady of the highest social position.

Dick. They all are. I never knew a music teacher that wasn't.

The century turned, and "guys" referring to men in general began to bloom. It was still slang, but no longer restricted to people of bad fortune or fashion.

Augustus Thomas wrote this line for a character in his 1902 comedy, *The Other Girl*:

> *You know they don't care what they say, these newspaper guys. (Pause) That sort of thing don't help a girl any.*

An article about modern young sailors in the November 1904 *Century* magazine by R. F. Zogbaum, "Our Modern Blue-Jacket," has this comment:

> *Although, with clue-garnets and stu'n'sails, much of the picturesque language of the sea has passed away, Jack's conversation is still garnished with expressions and terms born of the conditions of his life on the ocean. His language with his mates is a curious combination of Bowery slang and sea-phrases—"Youse* **guys** *come in out er that boat and bear a hand!"—as I heard one young cockswain order—and I believe that if Shakspere could have known our modern Yankee man-of-war's-man, he never would have put strange oaths in the mouth of a soldier.*

During the 1900s lower-class slang still predominates, as in these quotes from early 20th-century fiction:

> *"I ain't fer long, no how," less all them* **guys** *are ijuts. (1906)*

I'm going out to-night to see if there's any word from the—from the party. These **guys** *ain't all fools. (1907)*

After a while you come to long enough to hand your money to a man behind a little window who thrusts a ticket into your face and tells you to "git out o' de way an' give de odder **guys** *a chancet"—a thing which you couldn't help doing if you wanted to. (1907)*

Denver relaxed into a range song by way of repartee: "I want mighty bad to be married, To have a garden and a home; I ce'tainly aim to git married, And have a gyurl for my own.""Aw! Y'u fresh **guys** *make me tired."(1908, Wyoming)*

"We'll have the men we want inside of fifteen minutes,"he promised the mob. "We'll rush them from both sides, and show those **guys** *on the landing whether they can stop us,"added Bostwick. (Same as above)*

10

LADIES AND GENTLEMEN

We're all guys

By mid-20th century, "guy" and "guys," having made the transformation from Guy Fawkes to effigies of him and then to designating the lowest of male humans, gradually had expanded its domain to include not just lower-class or funny-looking or socially inept males but finally all males and all classes, with mild implications of camaraderie. Nobody planned or intended this expansion; it was just a natural development of a convenient word to its full extent. It helped that, being a slang word (or at least informal), it developed without being noticed by makers of dictionaries or grammar books, who might well have found fault with it. So "guy" today remains a widely used designation for anyone male, from infant to elder, from richer to poorer, from saintly to wicked, from any place or religion on the globe. Every male is a guy, and that's nice.

But the plural "guys" didn't stop even there. By the middle of the 20th century, it had expanded once more, to include women along with men in its embrace, indeed the whole human race. And that, in turn, made "guys" or "you guys" suddenly the leading candidate for the centuries-long vacancy in second-person plural pronouns advertised in Chapter 8.

Thanks to the Brigham Young University (BYU) database, Corpus of Historical American English (CHAE), we can trace the accelerating growth of "guys" and "you guys" in our language to the present day. In the CHAE sample of more than 400 million words, from 1810 to 2010, the CHAE found 1776 instances of "you guys," all of them dated 1910 or later. If there were earlier examples, CHAE didn't find them, perhaps because "you guys" was so informal or slangy that it would rarely appear in print. Where it did, it was mostly in dialogue in fiction or lines in a play. By the time the database was able to catch examples of it, "you guys" had begun to move toward respectability.

Specifically, decade by decade of the past century, CHAE finds in its database these numbers of "guys" and "you guys" (see Figure 10.1).

For the 21st century, BYU's Corpus of Contemporary American English, with more than 560 million words just for the years 1990–2017 (about 10 times as many words as CHAE for each decade), found 3748 examples from the 1990s, 5005 examples from the 2000s, and 6656 from the shorter period 2010 to 2017.

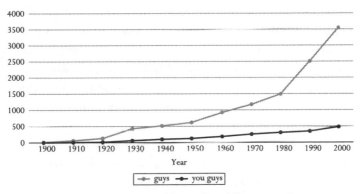

FIGURE 10.1 Frequency of "guys" and "you guys"
Source: Corpus of Historical American English, Brigham Young University

And in the 14 billion words of BYU's new iWeb Corpus, "you guys" appears 351,905 times, or about once every 40,000 words. "You guys," along with plain "guys," is at home in present-day American English, encompassing not just males and females but everyone else considered human, including GLBTQs.

It's easy to understand why this expansion happened. "Guy," from the beginning and through all expanded uses, remained solidly male, a characteristic of the word going back to its original, the definitely male Guy Fawkes. But "guys" was different. It was used in the 19th century to refer to groups. These were groups of males at first. But in many such groups, occasionally a female would be included.

Here's a 1911 example, from *Dawn O'Hara, The Girl Who Laughed,* the first novel by Edna Ferber, who later won a Pulitzer Prize for her novel *So Big.* It's only one instance, and the author doesn't call attention to it. If she had made a fuss about it, that might have elicited criticism. But she didn't, and in fact it appears that she didn't notice anything special about it. It slipped under the radar without comment.

The narrator of the story is Dawn herself, telling of her experience working in New York City as a journalist, a mostly male occupation at that time. Her colleagues on the newspaper are all men. In a hospital one of them, Blackie, is dying after an automobile accident. Dawn is the one woman among five colleagues summoned to the hospital for a quick farewell. Blackie says "you guys" to this audience of one woman and four men:

> *I met them in the stiff little waiting room of the hospital—*
> *Norberg, Deming, Schmidt, Holt—men who had known*
> *him from the time when they had yelled, "Heh, boy!" at*
> *him when they wanted their pencils sharpened. . . .*
>
> *A nurse in stripes and cap appeared in the doorway.*
> *She looked keenly at the little figure in the bed. Then she*
> *turned to us. "You must go now," she said. "You were just to*
> *see him for a minute or two, you know." Blackie summoned*
> *the wan ghost of a smile to his lips. "Guess* **you guys**
> *ain't got th' stimulatin' effect that a bunch of live wires*
> *ought to have." . . .*

> *They said good-by, awkwardly enough. Not one of them that did not owe him an unpayable debt.*

From 1911, also, we find a play by Rachel Crothers titled "He and She" that has "guys" entirely female, in the phrase "wise guys":

MILLICENT. Oh, mother, don't be cross. (Reaching a hand up to her mother's arm.) Sit down and talk a minute.

HERFORD. It's late. You must—

MILLICENT. That's nothing. We girls often talk till twelve.

HERFORD. Till twelve? Do the teachers know it?

MILLICENT. (Laughing again.) Oh, mother, you're lovely! Do the teachers know it? Why, don't you suppose they know that they don't know everything that's going on? They're pretty **wise guys** those ladies—they know when to let you alone. That's why the school's so popular.

"Guys" also can apply when the "group" consists of just two, one man and one woman. It's in the dialogue for a 1930 movie by Earl Baldwin and Ruth Rankin, *The Widow from Chicago*:

(The two gunmen stare sheepishly at each other. Crestfallen, they slowly put away their guns. Mullins and Polly dance into the scene. Both he and Polly are grinning.)

MULLINS. (lightly) Don't get excited, boys. It's all in fun.

FIRST GUNMAN. (huffed) Yeah? **You guys** got a swell sense of humor.

(Mullins and Polly laugh.)

Sinclair Lewis provides another example of inclusive "you guys" in his 1938 novel *Prodigal Parents*. Sara, the 28-year-old daughter of a car dealer in upstate New York and a graduate of Vassar, is attracted to Gene, a radical revolutionary, who says to her, "Nobody comes through with funds for the revolution like the wives of millionaires, even after we've openly announced we intend to overthrow the Democratic State and institute a real, honest-to-God dictatorship of the rednecks like me. How come? You're a capitalist, darling. Why do **you guys** in the ruling class let us get away with it?"

In 1945, writer Elma Lobaugh used "you guys" for a male–female couple in her mystery novel, *She Never Reached the Top*. Jennie, who arrives with Jim, is the narrator:

> *Jim honked the horn and a minute or two later light streamed out of the garage doors to the right of the house. And when I heard Bernard's loud voice I had to laugh at the thought of the ghost of a fragile girl haunting any house where he lived. "Thought* **you guys** *were never going to get here. How're you, Jennie? That blonde you liked couldn't come this week end, Jim. Here, let me take those bags."*

As the 20th century progressed, the use of "guys" to mean everyone was becoming more and more pervasive. Nobody was advocating it; it just seemed the normal and usually positive way to refer to a group of at least two humans. Rita Salz, a resident of Princeton, New Jersey, and formerly of Connecticut and West

Virginia, in a November 2018 message attested to the female use of "guys" and "you guys" as far back as the mid-20th century:

> *My undergraduate years began in Autumn 1956, at Smith College. Those were the days before transgender (except for someone named Christine Jorgensen), so we students were female females. And "you guys" was the common phrase for addressing a group of fellow students.*
>
> *In fact, I recall one event in which the use of the phrase was called into question. The occasion was the wedding of a Smith friend a class or two ahead of me. It was a kind of wedding I'd only read about, held at the Greenwich, Connecticut home of the bride's parents with the wedding party in formal wear (which did not stop the groomsmen from shoving one another, fully-clad, into the classic pool, after the ceremony). The bridesmaids and many, perhaps most, of the bride's friends were Smithies. One of the groomsmen overheard a "Hey, you guys," from a late-arriving Smithie, and took her to task for using the phrase in addressing a gaggle of girls.*
>
> *He was ignored. But I assure you, "you guys" was common parlance among us at Smith, in the late 1950's.*

Another recent correspondent wrote,

> *"Guy" may be gendered, but "you guys" certainly denoted a group without reference to gender when I was growing*

> *up in New York State and Pennsylvania. Have heard it*
> *for decades used in groups of girls or women, calling to*
> *other girls / women.*

In response to a post by Erin McKean on the Language Log website in 2010, "Julie" wrote:

> *As another Californian, I agree [that "you guys" is not*
> *new in California.] I've said it for about 50 years, and*
> *my mother (nearly 80) uses it unconsciously, just as I do.*
> *It's a set phrase, and applies to groups of both sexes. (For*
> *the record, I doubt I have ever said "you boys," or "you girls"*
> *for any reason. Those, to me, sound demeaning if not re-*
> *ferring to children.)*

By the later 20th century inclusive "you guys" was absolutely routine. In *The Fan Club* (1974) by Irving Wallace, for example, set in Los Angeles, a 9-year-old daughter addresses her parents as "you guys." The father narrates:

> *the children will be in from playing soon, hungry and*
> *dirty. Like our marriage, I think, hungry and dirty. While*
> *I ate the Grape Nuts, Natasha and Sean came in, brown*
> *arms and legs and blond hair crowding through the door*
> *at once, the screen slamming behind them. Natasha is*
> *nine; she is the love child who bound us. Sean is seven.*
> *Looking at them I felt love for the first time that day.*

> *"You slept late," Sean said.*
>
> *"That's because you were up late,* **you guys** *were fighting," Natasha said. "I heard you."*

Around the English-speaking world, "you guys" continues to grow. That's the case in England, home of the original Guy, and as far away as Australia. Canadian linguist Sali Tagliamonte noted in March 2018 about the English city of York, the home town of Guy Fawkes:

> *I have just returned from a field trip to York England with a team of 7 students. We spent the week doing sociolinguistic interviews—47 in all! Now we will be conducting a 4 x 4 comparison of intensifiers in York (1997) and York (2018) compared to Toronto (2003) and Toronto (2018). The idea is to "Catch Language Change."*
>
> *One thing I noticed that was quite striking. When I moved to York in 1997 the use of "you guys" for 2nd person plural was unheard of in York. When I used it with my classes of young men and women they would pretty much fall on the floor laughing. This trip, I heard so many people using "you guys." It has taken over!*

Nowadays, despite its masculine origin, "guys" or its equivalent "you guys" is heard increasingly worldwide where English is spoken, and in particular in the United States, as a second-person plural pronoun referring to any group of two or more. In fact, it is so frequent and so normal, most of the time we don't notice that we are saying it. We can tell it has become the norm because we almost always use it without thinking.

Well, with a few exceptions, as the next chapter acknowledges.

11

ROADBLOCKS

Feminist and Southern objections

Little attention has been paid to the pervasive spread of "guy" and "you guys" in recent times, even though in the 21st century it has defeated its rivals to take its prominent place among the personal pronouns of English. For the success of "guys" in this context, the lack of notice is a good thing, perhaps equivalent to the lack of attention to the activities of the Gunpowder Treasoners that allowed their plot to come so close to fruition.

Throughout the centuries, there seems to have been no noticeable objection to the word "guy" itself, even though it originally referred to the demonic and terrifying villain Guy Fawkes, and then gradually came to refer to men of the lowest class. As it spread, in America in particular, it shed awareness of its despicable early referents, allowing it to put on the mantle of informal conversation. In that way it was like America's greatest word, OK, which became respectable and indispensable only after its origin as a dimwitted deliberate misspelling of the initials of "all correct" was forgotten.

So "guy" and "guys" were a success before they faced criticism. But face it they finally did, and the opposition hasn't ceased.

The first stern objection came in the latter 20th century, from feminists who noticed the inherent sexism of the English language. It was so inherent, so normal, that rarely, if ever, had it been brought to everyone's intention that using "man" to designate both males and females meant implicit subordination of females, who were invisible in statements intended to include them, like "all men are created equal." That also implicated words beginning or ending with "-man," like "mankind," "fireman," "policeman," and "chairman."

Calling attention to this gender bias has resulted in efforts to make our language truly gender neutral, by deleting sexist vocabulary and replacing it as needed. That works well when a familiar synonym is available. We are used to saying "firefighter," "police officer," "chair." It's harder when the synonym isn't so readily available, as, for example, in the case of "freshman." It contains the unquestionably sexist "man" but with the emphasis on the first syllable, the gender-neutral "fresh" that would be lost if the word were replaced by "first-year student." That replacement therefore is not always made, even by some who generally favor gender neutrality.

Along came "guy" and "guys," then, always strongly associated with males. And, for some even in the present day, occasionally with lower-class or uncultivated males. While, under feminist pressure, other masculine words were receding in actual usage, "guy" and "guys" were merrily rolling along with little interference. "Guys" was calmly reaching out to swallow humanity whole, while "guy" provided a sharp contrast, remaining decidedly male.

It's one of the "pet peeves" that lexicographer Erin McKean wrote about for *the Boston Globe* in 2010. There's "a perceived gender disconnect," she observed, offering this example: "The waiter wouldn't address a group of men and women with 'you gals,' so why should he or she use 'you guys'? This may shortly be followed by another kind of indignation: 'Do I look like a guy?'" Or, she adds, "'You guys' may simply make some women feel overlooked or ignored, especially a single woman in a group being addressed as 'you guys.'"

When it was reprinted in the Linguist List blog later that year, McKean's column elicited more than 100 responses. Among them:

> *I would guess that the waitress who said "you guys" to older people was probably young and to her the phrase was normal for addressing a group informally, while the listener who thought it was demeaning was probably at least middle-aged. Conversely, to me, "you folks" in that situation would have sounded condescending on the part of the young waitress, "talking down" to the older folks by using their own idiom! (marie lucie)*

And another wrote:

> *for everyone that says "you guys" is gender neutral, how
> come all these articles out there have headings like "How
> to make GUYS want you," "What GUYS mean when they
> say. . . ."*
>
> *You CANNOT have the same word that you are clearly
> using for males to be gender inclusive unless you accept
> the fact that it's the same as using MEN for a group of
> people of either gender or female only.*
>
> *Don't tell me people who use "You Guys" don't know
> what they are saying, as I hear many people dropping
> the YOU and just saying GUYS! to get people's atten-
> tion . . . and guess what . . . people who actually
> THINK and give a damn about language and are
> not brainwashed to thinking something black is really
> white, they have every right to comment and ignore
> people who use this type of logic. BTW for those who
> can't think of anything other than "You Guys" try "You
> All," "Everyone" "You 2, 3, 4 (whatever number of people
> you are referring to," "You Folks," "Friends," "We" . . . and
> many more. . . . Try using your brain and not being
> so lazy!*

If only language were logical, this argument would be hard to
refute. It's difficult to make a logical case against her reasoning
that a word can't be masculine in the singular and gender neutral

in the plural. But language doesn't work that way. It's conventional, not logical. Nowadays we hear "guy" a lot referring to any male, and "guys" a lot referring to every human. Convention trumps logic. So if we want to avoid saying "guys" to a group of women, it's as difficult as it is to keep to a strict diet when everyone else is eating cake.

And just as logically, you could look at it another way, as a triumph for feminists. You could argue that "guys" shows women conquering territory that had been exclusively male. It's like women gaining full membership in a previously all-male club. Who is the conqueror? Or is it a matter of conquest at all?

Nowadays, in any case, despite its masculine origin, "you guys" or its equivalent "guys" is heard in English worldwide as a second-person plural pronoun. For most of the English-speaking world, and certainly for North America, it has become the conventional way for one person to call for the attention of others regardless of gender. We can tell it has become the norm because we almost always use it without thinking.

Y'all

Another alternative to "guys" or "you guys" is the well-known "y'all." It's the norm in the Old South, encompassing Virginia in the east to Texas in the west, and Tennessee, Arkansas, and Oklahoma to the north. The South lost the Civil war, but not "y'all." If anything, "y'all" now seems stronger than ever, perhaps the single most prominent feature of southern speech.

When you hear "y'all," you know you're in the South, or else visiting with a southerner in some northern place. "Y'all" has the advantage over "you guys" of seeming both friendly and polite, and of not being considered slang. "Guys" can now enter through the front door rather than having to beg at the back, but only "y'all" is welcome even in the parlor.

Evidence of "y'all" goes back half a century before evidence of "you guys" in the *Oxford English Dictionary*. The OED cites a humorous story in the *Southern Literary Messenger* in 1859 by "Mozis Addums" (George William Bagby), writing about his life in a boarding house in Washington, DC:

> *Packin uv pork in a meet house, which you should*
> *be keerful it don't git hot at the bone, and prizin uv*
> *tobakker, which y'all's Winstun nose how to do it, givs*
> *you a parshil idee, but only parshis.*

The first three of 574 "y'all"s in the Corpus of Historical American English (CHAE) are in a single passage also by Bagby, where a Virginian imagines how he would spend $50 million benevolently in his home state. Here he reflects on the many men he has known:

"Did y'all know Woody Latham?" said I. And they answered and said they did.

"We desire some pizen," they added.

"Did y'all know Judge Semple?" said I. They answered yes, and most of them lied. "And did y'all know Jim McDonald and Bob Ridgway and Chas. Irving and Marcellus Anderson and Philander McCorkle."

More evidence comes in Edward Eggleston's *Queer Stories for Boys and Girls* (1884):

> *Then he drew the revolver, carefully examined the chambers to see that all were filled; motioned with his hand to those on the ground, saying, quietly, "Pick those up. Y'all may need every one of 'em." The Blue Grass dialect seemed cropping out the stronger for his preoccupation.*

Finally, in 1886 S. Pardee wrote for *Dixie*, published in Atlanta, about "Odd Southernisms: A Few Examples of Quaint Sayings in South Carolina".

> *"You all," or, as it should be abbreviated, "y'all," is one of the most ridiculous of all the Southernisms I can call to mind.*

These are the database numbers from CHAE for "y'all," decade by decade (see Figure 11.1).

For some time, "y'all" has been assaulted by "you guys" aiming to replace it as the go-to second-person plural pronoun in the South. The South may have lost the Civil War, but to this day it seems to hold off the northern "you guys." Is the Solid South still

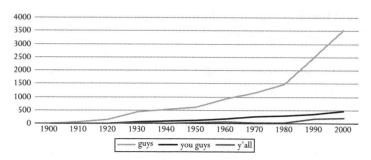

FIGURE II.I Frequency of "y'all," "guys," and "you guys"
Source: Corpus of Historical American English, Brigham Young University

really holding firm at the Mason-Dixon line, or is "you guys"
infiltrating and spreading like kudzu, as it is elsewhere?

Some claim that it is. In the *Dictionary of American Regional
English* (DARE), the usage note for "you guys" says "orig. chiefly
North; now widespread; esp freq. among younger speakers." It
backs this up with two citations that suggest the invasion has been
on its way at least since the recent turn of the century:

> *2000 American Speech 75.417: Meanwhile, just as
> y'all seems to be spreading outside the South, you-
> guys is moving into the South, especially among
> younger speakers. [Quoting a 1999 survey by Natalie
> Maynor, which continues: "In a survey of university
> students in Mississippi, Alabama, North Carolina,
> and South Carolina, I found a surprisingly large*

> *number of respondents who said that they might use*
> *you-guys."]*

And DARE quotes a 2002 article in *Alcalde* from central Texas:

> *From this office . . . you can hear it in the classrooms, at*
> *the shuttle bus stops. "You guys know where this stops?"You*
> *can hear it in the bookstores and restaurants that encircle*
> *campus. "You guys know what you want to order yet?" I'm*
> *speaking, of course, about the impending death of the*
> *expression "y'all" at the hands of the address "you guys,"*
> *like an aggressive exotic species supplanting a native one.*

Nevertheless, at the end of the second decade of the 21st century, the South seems to be holding on to "y'all." In July 2018, wondering about the current situation, I invited readers of the Lingua Franca blog of the *Chronicle of Higher Education* to report from the field. The responses suggested little change from the situation in 2000. This is a typical response:

> *Here in southeast Missouri I have to say I think it has be-*
> *come a standoff, as some generations are standing strong*
> *with "y'all" and "all y'all", I do have to say I am hearing*
> *more and more younger generations using "you guys."*
>
> *I'm from the upper South—Fayetteville, Ark.—and*
> *still hear "y'all" considerably more frequently than "you*
> *guys," which I started hearing in Fayetteville as early*

as the mid-1970s. It very likely came via friends with parents who arrived here from points north to teach at the University of Arkansas, so the kudzu has deep roots.

But people who do use "you guys" here almost blush after saying it for some sense that it sounds uncouth or gendered, very often apologizing and clarifying they meant "all of you" or "you all," without the contraction.

Recently, I thought perhaps "y'all" was on the rise after I attended the state mathematics quiz bowl—further south in the state—and heard the organizer congratulating the attendees for their participation: "All y'all give all y'allselves a round of applause." (Charlie Alison)

And from the Sunshine State:

I'm from Florida, where we joke that the further south you go, the further north you are. Among the transplants and snowbirds, "you guys" is definitely more common, unless they're trying to be ironic. From true Floridians, however, I still hear "ya'll" used frequently, even among students.

I also feel like I heard "you guys" more in the 90s than I do now, although that could be the result of having been on a college campus with a diverse national and international student body. I'm now at a small college that serves a more local population. Personally, I use "ya'll" in conversation, but have always felt weird typing/writing it, and in those instances tend to use "you."

And one more:

> *Southern Alabama here. Y'all is still the dominant form*
> *but I do hear you guys from younger folks and transplants*
> *occasionally (usually transplants do a pretty good job*
> *of picking up y'all). I especially hear it from servers in*
> *restaurants, maybe because they feel it's more formal*
> *somehow? It drives me crazy because not only does it*
> *not feel formal to me, it doesn't even feel friendly like*
> *y'all does.*
>
> *But, I also hear y'all being used more and more from*
> *northerners too, and not just AAVE [African American*
> *Vernacular English] speakers but folks from predomi-*
> *nantly white areas like Vermont. It will be interesting to*
> *see how it turns out in 50 years or so.*

But I'll leave the last word to the preeminent scholar of Southern American English, Michael Montgomery of the University of South Carolina, writing recently:

> *Yes, you guys has been making steady inroads in the*
> *South over the past 30–40 years (the period of my ob-*
> *servation). When growing up, I recall that even the noun*
> *guy 'fellow' had a slightly crude tinge of disrespect for*
> *any male to whom it was applied. As an East Tennessean*
> *with Deep South parents, all I ever heard was y'all (and*
> *occasionally you all). These two pronouns (along with*
> *various periphrastic forms such as you two or you fellows)*

represented default usage. You guys was unknown as a pronoun, and to include females it was inconceivable.

I can vividly remember sitting close to a lad of 10–12 and his parents at an airport gate maybe 30 years ago and being shocked to hear him address his parents as you guys. I also recall going to a restaurant with my aunt and uncle c1995 and my uncle's visible excruciation when the young server miss queried "what can I get you guys tonight?" At the very least, the pronoun communicated a chumminess that I regarded as entirely inappropriate.

And he adds:

I'm not nearly as sanguine about the resistance to you guys as I once was. I still hear double modals nearly every week with the same pragmatics as ever, and speakers seem oblivious to using them.[1]

But I hear you guys as well, though I don't like it! And I'm sure that tens of millions of Americans who grew up with y'all now have switched.

1. Montgomery explains double modals:

[In 2018] a physical therapist said to me, "Since it's not five o'clock yet, I *might can* get hold of them before they close," whereupon I asked the young fellow about his roots. He responded "Charleston, South Carolina." In other words, he expressed possibility without claiming to speak for someone not already consulted and about whom he was unsure. He was hedging, not making a promise he *might couldn't* fulfill himself.

12

VILLAIN BECOMES HERO

The Modern Guy Fawkes

Modern guises and disguises of the original Guy

But what about Guy Fawkes? As "guy" and "guys" become ever more familiar, is he remembered as the original Guy, or is he left behind?

The answer is definitely the latter, at least for the United States and in some instances at least also the rest of the English-speaking world.

During the 20th century, most users of "guy" and "guys" had not the slightest awareness of its connection to Fawkes. Severing the connection, in fact, was necessary to allow the word to acquire positive connotations. Toward the end of that century, however, as the original reason for bonfires on November 5 faded from memories even in England, the face of Guy Fawkes became more familiar than ever.

This was thanks to *V for Vendetta*, a graphic novel written by Alan Moore, illustrated by David Lloyd. It began as a serial in an obscure comic in England in 1982. The finished story was published in one volume by DC Comics in 1988.

V for Vendetta imagines a Labour electoral victory in the 1980s that develops into a ruthless Fascist government in the 1990s, one that keeps the population in thrall by television propaganda and ruthless force. Opposing the entire Fascist regime is a lone rebel, who develops skill with all manner of weapons as he miraculously manages to escape from a government concentration camp. He calls himself simply V, the V standing for Vendetta as in the title. And he goes about single-handedly destroying the entire government, thus freeing the population of England and enabling an anarchist state.

Moore and Lloyd made this character a modern Guy Fawkes. In the very first chapter, after rescuing a young woman from sexual assault and worse by government police, V recites to her the familiar "Remember, remember, the fifth of December, gunpowder, treason, and plot. I know of no reason why gunpowder treason should ever be forgot." And with that they watch as the houses of Parliament blow up, followed by a V in fireworks.

What is particularly memorable about the character of V is his costume: a cloak with daggers, a hat like the fashionable one depicted in contemporary illustrations of Guy Fawkes, and a face mask that is a simplified version of Guy's face in those contemporary illustrations. The one difference is the smug smile on V's mask. The smile changes the original Guy's fierce look to a light-hearted cheerful one, making him appear to be laughing as he goes about terrifying and destroying officers of the Fascist regime.

After a year of successful surprise attacks, the government collapses and freedom reigns. V himself dies, but the young woman puts on his mask and arranges a "Viking funeral" for V, complete with blowing up the prime minister's residence on Downing Street.

This Guy Fawkes mask reached a larger audience in the 2006 movie made from the book, featuring Natalie Portman as a much stronger version of Evey and Hugo Weaving as V. The time moves ahead to remain in the near future. The destruction of the Houses of Parliament takes place in modern fashion: In a disused line of the Underground, V sends an empty subway train filled with explosives under the building. This makes for a grand finale of explosions and fireworks amid Tchaikovsky's *1812 Overture*, witnessed by angry citizens in the streets, all wearing Guy masks. The movie was changed so much that Moore refused to endorse it or have anything to do with it. But the connection to Guy Fawkes remains, and so does the mask.

Both the novel and the movie represent the complete transformation of Guy Fawkes from diabolic arch-villain of 1605 to heroic freedom fighter of the present day. Both versions explicitly refer to the original Guy, thus adopting the original Guy's attitude toward evil authority, and making him succeed where the original Guy did not.

Unlike his collaborator Moore, David Lloyd approved of the movie. He told BBC:

> *The Guy Fawkes mask has now become a common brand and a convenient placard to use in protest against tyranny, and I'm happy with people using it. It seems quite unique, an icon of popular culture being used this way. My feeling is the Anonymous group needed an all-purpose image to hide their identity and also symbolize that they stand for individualism.*
>
> *V for Vendetta is a story about one person against the system. We knew that V was going to be an escapee from a concentration camp where he had been subjected to medical experiments but then I had the idea that in his craziness he would decide to adopt the persona and mission of Guy Fawkes, our great historical revolutionary.*

As Lloyd said, the book and the movie made the Guy Fawkes mask an icon for protests against governments and institutions perceived as evil. During the Occupy Wall Street movement of September 2011 and subsequent "we are the 99 percent" protests against wealth and income inequality, some protestors wore V masks to show their determination and unity, as well as to conceal their identity.

The masks are made by a variety of companies in a variety of styles, but the mask used in the movie is copyrighted by Time Warner and earns a royalty on every mask sold. It's also a popular mask for Halloween.

The book and the movie today are the best-known current versions of Guy Fawkes, but they weren't the first. The change in attitudes toward the original Guy began about 200 years ago. Early in the 19th century, James Sharpe notes, Fawkes sometimes had a role other than simply the villain of a dramatic or literary work.

In 1835, for example, the "comic pantomime" called "Harlequin and Guy Fawkes: Or the 5th of November" had its premiere at Theatre Royal Covent Garden. A character named "Winter Discontent" gets Fawkes's help in blowing up the House of Parliament:

> *A swaggering roaring boisterous invader*
> *That came to England in the famed Armada*
> *Who fears not for Reformers or hard knocks*
> *A man of metal true called Guido Fawkes*

With pantomime and rhymes like that, it's hard to be frightened by this caricature of Guido.

In the mid-19th century, Guy Fawkes was a character in another pantomime comedy, "Guy Fawkes or a Match for a King." The plot is updated to modern times, with the chief plotter

Catesby now a director of the Accidental Death Insurance Company, worried about having to pay life insurance for a character who would be likely to attend the opening of Parliament. Catesby writes him a warning letter. "What is totally lacking," Sharpe says, "is any reference to the more serious undertones of the Plot."

> *When crackling faggots make the bonfire hot,*
> *Let prejudice with faggots be faggot, [sic]*
> *And let tar barrels with their roasting ribs,*
> *Present the only objects for your squibs.*
> *Let old antipathies in crackers end,*
> *And polemic with fire balloons ascend.*

In quick order in the 19th century, Guy Fawkes changed from villain to hero in works of drama and fiction. It helped that Catholics were no longer the enemy.

In 1840, in the novel "Guido Fawkes: Or, the Prophetess of Ordsall Cave," Fawkes appears as a champion of the poor against "haughty masters." "Ye look upon the poor as slaves," this Fawkes says in one of his milder lines, "and set up rulers over them; any law you make is but to keep them more in subjection." And he concludes, "Ye are going full gallop to the devil!"

William Harrison Ainsworth's 1841 novel *Guy Fawkes, or the Gunpowder Treason: An Historical Romance* keeps Fawkes in the role of plotter but he is sympathetic, including a love match leading to marriage. As he prepares for the explosion, he declares, "Men cannot read my heart, but heaven can; and the sincerity of my purpose will be recognised above."

As the 19th century goes on, Guy Fawkes becomes more distant and less important, for example, in the 1888 novel *Return of the Native* by Thomas Hardy. The background for the first day of the narrative happens to be November 5, where on Egdon Heath that evening some 30 fires are lit by furze carriers. That would seem to be a remembrance of Guy Fawkes, but Hardy spurns that interpretation as too modern:

> *It was as if these men and boys had suddenly dived into past ages, and fetched therefrom an hour and deed which had before been familiar with this spot. The ashes of the original British pyre which blazed from that summit lay fresh and undisturbed in the barrow beneath their tread. The flames from funeral piles long ago kindled there had shone down upon the lowlands as these were shining now. Festival fires to Thor and Woden had followed on the same ground and duly had their day. Indeed, it is pretty well known that such blazes as this the heathmen were now enjoying are rather the lineal descendants from jumbled Druidical rites and Saxon ceremonies than the invention of popular feeling about Gunpowder Plot.*

To this day a flicker of interest in the original Guy remains, more in England than in the America that threw off its allegiance to the British crown. But it's now completely separate from the ordinary words "guy" and "guys" we use every day. And so, guys, it's time to get back to the rest of the story of those transformed words.

13

GUYS VICTORIOUS

Resistance is futile

For two centuries, as we have noted in Chapter 8, an important position in the English language remained vacant. It was the second-person plural pronoun, needed to make clear that we are addressing more than one person. The vacancy began, however, not with the plural second-person "ye, you, yours" but with the singular "thou, thee, thine," which those who spoke English had gradually more and more been avoiding. Something had to take the place of the singular, and in fact something already had been replacing the missing "thou": the plural "you," seen as a more polite form of address to one person.

That was not so satisfactory. It meant that "you," heretofore only a plural, now was a singular too. In the second person, as a result, there was no way to tell a singular from a plural. A distinctive form had to be added in order to allow the distinction once more,

Incidentally, that's also the case with the similar problem of finding a third-person singular pronoun for English that is gender neutral—something to take the place of "he" or "she" to avoid the sexism we have recently been alerted to. "It" won't do because it's not human. "They" is gender neutral but plural. After two centuries of proposals like "s/he" or "qi," some authorities like the editors of the *Oxford English Dictionary* recently settled on extending "they" to refer to one person as well as more than one.

The new second-person form could be a singular pronoun, but that would have meant trying something like "thou," which we had been pointedly avoiding in favor of its replacement "you." So the vacancy was for the plural. And the race was on to find a worthy replacement.

How would the replacement be determined? Not by decree or by logical deduction. Language generally isn't logical, it's just conventional, at least when know-it-all authorities aren't involved. And they weren't in this case. Nobody announced a competition for the second-person plural pronoun; nobody vetted proposals. Speakers and writers just used whatever came in their heads, usually not noticing the ad hoc circumstances that might call for particular choices of pronoun.

"Guys" in the 18th century was in no shape to be a candidate. It was too limited in scope, too low class, too vulgar, too slangy. The wisest scholar of language in that century could not imagine it would be a possible solution to the problem.

Among the viable candidates were ones we consider non-standard nowadays. One obvious candidate involved the simple addition of the suffix –s to make "you" plural, with the spelling "yous" or "youse." Another possibility was "you ones," spelled and pronounced "you-uns" or more concisely "yinz."

Phrases could be candidates: "you folks" or "you people," for example, but the first is a little too folksy for all situations and the second is a little too distant sometimes. And other such phrases, like "you citizens" or "you children," are much too limited to be used in all situations.

An important possibility was "you all" or "y'all," both still in use, the latter predominant in the Old South. "You all" is perfectly fine for formal speech or writing but a little stiff for everyday conversation. "Y'all" is fine for everyday conversation but a little too informal for solemn occasions.

So the second-person pronoun box remained empty for a good two centuries. That was so long that "guys" had time to gradually expand to meet the criteria that would satisfy users. During that time it managed to shift its connotations 180 degrees, from nasty to nice, from evil to benevolent. Not that "guys" was ever officially declared to have met the criteria for second-person plural, and not that there ever were officials involved, and not that users were ever aware there was a competition—except perhaps in the case of "y'all."

What "guys" succeeded in doing, once its scope had expanded to include everybody, was to make a clear distinction between singular and plural in the second-person pronouns. Whether you said "you guys" or "you," in either case the –s at the end clearly made it a plural, clearly in contrast with the singular "guy," which wasn't a candidate for the singular. The second-person pronouns in this situation, then, were "you" clearly just in the singular and "guys" or "you guys" just in the plural. Problem solved, "guys" ensconced.

Another quality that helped "guy" and "guys" throughout its ascent was its quasi-invisibility. It could develop meanings naturally as contexts changed, without interference from lexicographers, grammarians, schoolteachers, and other authorities.

Linguists make a distinction between *unmarked* and *marked* words. In any sentence or discourse, we usually pay little attention to the words we use or hear. Paying attention to particular words would distract from the message we are trying to convey, so in most cases we try to use the most normal vocabulary. Those words are *unmarked*. The words that distract us from our message are *marked*. It's not that either kind is better, just that they have different roles in a sentence. Putting a word in a marked situation draws the listener's and reader's attention. (And a particular word can be marked in one context, unmarked in another.)

Viewed this way, "guys" has the advantage of being unmarked. We don't stop to think, Why did that guy use "guys"? It's simply the unmarked second-person plural pronoun we all know by heart. And in fact, all the basic elements of English or of any other language are unmarked. If they are marked, distracting someone every time they are used, conversations will be derailed.

It's especially curious to have attracted so little notice, when it has made a person's name into a personal pronoun. Never before has this been done in English.

In contrast, "y'all" is often highly marked. It's like flying a Confederate flag announcing, "I'm Southern." What do you think, y'all? Doesn't it stand out as a marked word, at least in that sentence? Contrast that with What do you think, you guys?

There's one other disadvantage to "y'all" as a second-person pronoun. Very simply, it can be ambiguous. Some people use it in the singular as well as the plural, once again blurring the distinction. "Y'all" has two strong indications of plural, "y-" being an abbreviation of "you," and "all" in other contexts making clear it's plural: "You all should get some sleep" is close to y'all should get some sleep (Plural? Singular? Too confusing).

So the game is over. "You guys" has made it to the unmarked center of the language. Resistance is futile.

But who has won? The terrorist Guy Fawkes, after all? The women who have extended the range of a very masculine word to encompass everyone? Or just everyone, now, who has the privilege to routinely and for the most part unconsciously use "you guys"? Or maybe all three?

14

FUTURE GUYS

It's up to us

So at last, guys, here we are. We've seen the amazing past and triumphant present of guys. But not its future. That's because we can't.

As I write this, the first fifth of the 21st century is coming to an end. But not the history of "guys."

In the previous chapters we've watched as "guys" had its birth in the given name of the most shocking terrorist England has ever known; its surprising endurance and then prominence as a by-product of an act of Parliament calling for annual thanksgiving ceremonies thanking God for forestalling the terrorist attempt; the gradual drift from proper name to generic over the centuries; its harsh treatment by George Washington; its use by some in the lower ranks of society; its spread across class and gender boundaries; its intrusion into the English pronoun system gradually filling the gap left by a vanished second-person plural pronoun, until—well, here we are in the present day, and here with us is "guys" in several prominent modern guises.

We have also digressed into the graphic novel *V for Vendetta*, inspired by the Guy of the Gunpowder Plot, and the feature film made from it; the mask worn by the revolutionary hero of *V for Vendetta*, inspired by a depiction of the original Guy, and adopted by Occupy protesters in the early 21st century. But since the revolutionary situations imagined and depicted by these modern derivatives have little to do with either the original plot or Bonfire Day, they are not part of the chain of evidence leading from the Guy to "you guys." In fact, essential to the present wide use of "guy" and "guys" is total separation from Guy Fawkes.

If Alan Moore had never written *V for Vendetta*, and if David Lloyd had never created the modern mask, and if the Occupy marchers of the current century had never worn the mask—the miraculous transformation of Guy Fawkes into "guy" and "you guys" would have proceeded undisturbed. So we haven't spent much time on those modern versions of protest inspired by Guy Fawkes. They are sidetracks, not the main line.

In short, this book has tried to do justice to the miraculous past and triumphant present of "guys." But what next? Does "guys" indeed have a future? Just listen to those around you if you have any doubt (and if you don't live in the South). Like a whirlwind, or perhaps a blast of fresh air, at the moment "guys" is gaining momentum, taking no prisoners as it has swept away other candidates for second-person plural pronoun.

If the story of "guys" has taught us anything, it's that the future of a language is not only unpredictable but sometimes unimaginable. With that understanding, there's no harm in speculating, as long as it's clear that there's no formula or theory to back up the speculation. Here are some possible scenarios:

1. "Guys" could become even more firmly settled and acknowledged as the unmarked (but usually friendly) second-person plural pronoun. It should become so firmly established that grammar instruction in schools and teachers would finally recognize it and teach it as standard.

2. "Guy" in the singular might lose its restriction to designating males only, allowing sentences like "She's quite a guy!" that occasionally occur already.

3. Conversely, feminists and others could argue so strenuously against "guys" that women would be embarrassed to use it.

4. Student activists who now insist on being addressed by their choice of pronoun could take the example of Guy and make their own name the second-person pronoun to be used by everyone, not just toward them but toward everybody. If the student is Carmen, she could address her friends as "carmens" or "you carmens." That makes as much sense as calling everyone "guys," the only differences being that she's the one who invents it for herself, and she won't have

400 years to make it the new second-person plural for all. Meanwhile, though, her classmate Karl might be addressing his friends as "karls" and urging them to use that for all second-person plural occasions. There would be plenty of candidates, and only one possible winner.

As for what really will happen: "Guys," what you yourself do may well make the difference. Not that you can change a definition by declaring that you will do it; changes come from slight, usually accidental and unintended and unnoticed reinterpretations of the words we hear. When enough people shift a meaning in a certain direction, the norm moves. But "guys" has settled in most likely for a long time to come.

FURTHER READING:
NOTES ON SOURCES

Not surprisingly in this our 21st century, the internet has supplied many sources for this book. This is especially true in the case of the instantly famous and unendingly discussed story of the Gunpowder Plot. The information is general knowledge and easily discovered.

Most of my internet sources are readily and freely available to anyone, with a simple Google search. This is particularly true of primary sources, the numerous original documents from 1605 to the present, which are now available online without requiring travel to libraries or archives.

For example, the complete record of the trial of Guy Fawkes and his co-conspirators, some 5500 words, will show up as your first choice if you google "guy fawkes trial transcript." That's all you need. It will get you to this page, though when you can google there's no need to use the exact URL:

http://www.armitstead.com/gunpowder/gunpowder_trial.html

Likewise, the "House of Commons journal 1605" is accessible by using that title, which will lead directly to:

https://www.british-history.ac.uk/commons-jrnl/vol1/p256

Again, no need to bother with exact web addresses.

Still, there are also some very useful print sources.

The topics of religious strife in England begun by Henry VIII's displacement of the pope as head of the English church; the Gunpowder Plot, and the life and death in particular of Guy Fawkes all drew the immediate attention of historians as well as preachers, politicians, and the general public of England. They have continued to keep that attention from the day when events took place right to the present.

There have been, as a result, many in-depth studies of the events of November 5, 1605, the context for them, and their aftermath. In the first few chapters my book presents some of the Catholic–Protestant religious conflicts that led to the extreme plot of Gunpowder Treason. Then comes Guy's story, not presenting any new discoveries in such a thoroughly researched field but looking through the evidence to explain how his name was immediately on everyone's tongue. Even today the original Guy remains among the best known figures in English history.

For a long time, as long as English Catholics battled English Protestants, the histories and biographies were partisan, taking one side or the other, often to extremes. In their eyes Guy Fawkes was a devil or a saint, depending on which side the partisan favored. But after several centuries, as the animosity between Catholics and protestants finally subsided, historians began to move toward a middle road, more judiciously and less stridently weighing the morality of the circumstances that led to the near destruction of the government in 1605.

To provide the religious context, I have relied particularly on *A Brief History of the English Reformation* by Derek Wilson, published in 2012 by Constable & Robinson. Only on a topic so extensively studied would "brief" be justified in the title of a 452-page book that includes a 17-page bibliography.

For Guy himself, my resource often has been *Pity for the Guy* by John Paul Davis, published in 2010 by Peter Owen. This one has a bibliography of a mere nine pages. The first word of the title is an indication of the book's more balanced presentation, implying sympathy for Guy as well as for his intended victims.

Likewise very useful has been *Faith and Treason: The Story of the Gunpowder Plot* by Antonia Fraser, published in 1996 by Doubleday in the United States. This one is 347 pages, including 11 pages of bibliography. "A full bibliography is impractical for reasons of space," she notes. Her title likewise implies sympathy for both sides: Catholic faith, on the one hand, leading to what protestants saw as treason, on the other.

James Sharpe's *Remember, Remember: A Cultural History of Guy Fawkes Day* (Harvard University Press, 2005) gives an excellent overview of developments in England with regard to Guy after 1605.

For details of Bonfire Day in the United States, Kevin Q. Doyle's "Rage and Fury Which Only Hell Could Inspire: The Rhetoric and the Ritual of Gunpowder Treason in Early America," his Ph.D. dissertation at Brandeis in 2013, is full of helpful specifics, with excellent early illustrations as a bonus. It too is available on the internet, by searching with the last five words of the title. It's an open access document, available free.

My later chapters contain numerous examples of "guy" and "guys" in contexts showing the evolving development of the denotations and connotations of those words. Most of the examples come from another new kind of free internet source, the database that encompasses large amounts of print publications of the past and present.

Especially notable are the corpora available freely from Brigham Young University by googling "BYU corpora" or the simple URL corpus.byu.edu. At this writing there are more than 20 different BYU corpora. Of particular relevance for this book are the 400 million words in the Corpus of Historical American English, the 520 million words in the Corpus of Contemporary American English (1990–2015), and the 755 million words in Early English Books Online. There are also the 14 billion (yes, billion!) contemporary words in the iWeb Corpus of 95 carefully selected websites.

And corpora are available elsewhere on the web too: Google Books, Making of America books and journals, and many more, provide increasing opportunities to search for instances of particular words of any time period.

Personal pronouns (Chapter 8) and their history likewise have been extensively studied and explained in descriptions of English grammar, so I didn't need to consult specialized studies to be able to offer the basic information this chapter provides. If you want more detail, googling something like "English second-person pronoun history" will lead quickly to further explanations, starting with Wikipedia.

INDEX

Act of Supremacy, 21–22
Adams, John, 89–90
Ainsworth, William Harrison, 142–43
Alcott, Louisa May, 110
America the Beautiful, 102
American Civil War, 129
American patriotic songs, 100–3
American Revolution, 8, 86
American South, 129
annates, 21
annulment of marriage to
        Catherine, 13–21
Anti–Catholic sentiment, 79–80
Arthur, Prince 11

Babington Plot, 37
Barlow, William, sermon, 72–73
barrels of gunpowder, 46, 48
Bede, Venerable, 24–25
bin Laden, Osama, 67
biographies of Fawkes, 6
Boleyn, Anne, 20–21
bonfires, 68, 70, 71, 77–78
Boston bonfires, 87–88
Browne, George, 78

Canterbury celebration of November
        5, 74–75
Carew, Thomas, 105, 106
Catesby, Robert, 42–43, 44–45

Catherine of Aragon, 11
    annulment, 20–21
    marriages and children, 18
    unconsummated marriage, 20
Catholic Church, 27
Catholic emancipation, 26–27
Catholic England pre–Reformation, 9
Cecil, Robert, 49
colonial celebrations in America, 83
Commonwealth, 26–27
Corpus of Contemporary American
        English, 116
Corpus of Historical American
        English, 116
Crothers, Rachel, 119

Darling Clementine, 93–94
Davis, John Paul, 6
Decker, Thomas, 75
Declaration of the Seven Sacraments
        Against Martin Luther, 15
Defender of the Faith, 17
Deuteronomy, Book of 12
double modals, 136n1
Dowry of Mary, 10

Edward III, 9
effigies of Guy and Pope, 78–79, 80
Elizabeth I, 28, 35–38
English Reformation 9

Essex Rebellion, 38
explosion, 66–67
explosion force, 51

Faux, Guy, 78–79, 105
Fawkes no longer fear–inducing, 141
Fawkes, Guy
    appearance, 60–61
    arrested in cellar, 50
    birth and baptism, 33
    as Devil, 2, 62
    executed, 64
    expertise in explosions, 45
    Gunpowder Plot, 45
    interrogated, 50
    parents, 33–34
    or son of the Devil, 77
    Spanish Brigade, 39
    tried, 62–64
feminist objections, 126
Ferber, Edna, 118–19
Fidei Defensor, 17
Fifth November Act of Parliament, 69
fireworks, 69, 70, 74, 77–78
Fraser, Antonia, 6
freedom of religion, 23, 25–26
frequency of "guy" and "guys"
        increases, 116–17

Gawain and the Green Knight
        pronouns, 98
gender–neutral third person singular
        pronoun, 146
gender–neutral words, 126
Gettysburg Address, 92
GLBTQ guys, 3, 117
grammar, 91–92

Guido Fawkes, 31, 48, 53–54
Gunpowder Plot, 42, 43
Gunpowder Treason, 66
Gunpowder Treason Day, 69, 74
"guy" a disreputable man, 107
"guy" and "guys" develop in 20th
        century, 115–16
"guy" any man, 107
"guy" as slang, 113–14, 115
"guys" becomes standard second–person
        plural pronoun, 116
"guys" includes females, 117
"guys" plural 108–14
Guy (French name), 29
Guy (name), 65
Guy de Maupassant, 30–31
"guy" etymology, 30, 33
"guy" extends meanings, 104
Guy Fawkes mask, 138–39, 140–41
Guy of Warwick, 30

Hardy, Thomas, 143
Harte, Bret, 112
Hayman, Robert, 86
Hell, 61–62, 75, 76, 77, 86
Henry VII, 11
Henry VIII
    Defender of the Catholic faith, 14
    desires son, 18
    marriage to Catherine of Aragon, 13
    skilled in theology, 15
Herring, Francis, 76–77
historians, 4–5
Holbeche House, 60
holy week, 69
House of Lords cellar, 46, 47
House of Lords chamber, 45

Intelligent Design, 8
interrogation of Guy, 54–59

James I of England, 40–42, 54, 57–58, 64
Jamestown, 84–85
John Johnson, alias for Guy, 31–33, 53–54
Jonson, Ben, 75–76

Kemble, Frances Anne, 111
King James Bible, 100–1

language not logical, 128–29, 146
Leo X, Pope, 17
Leviticus, Book of 12, 20
Lewis, Sinclair 120
Lloyd, David, 138, 140
Lopez Plot, 38
Luther, Martin 13–14

marked and unmarked words, 148–49
marriage to brother's widow,
    Biblical 12–13
Massachusetts, 83–84
McKean, Erin, 122, 127
Middle English pronouns, 97
Milton, John, 76
Monteagle, Lord, 48–49
Montgomery, Michael, 129–36
Moore, Alan, 138
My country, 'tis of thee, 101–2

Nash, Thomas, 61–62
Nero, Roman emperor, 72–73
Newfoundland, 86
9/11 attack on U.S., 51
Nixon, Richard, 92–93
Northern Rising, plot, 37

Observance of Fifth November
    Act, 68–69
Old English pronouns, 97
Papal excommunication of Elizabeth,
    28, 35–36
Parry Plot, 37
pennies for the guy, 107
Percy, Thomas, 31–32, 45
Peter's Pence, 21
Pius VI, Pope, 35–36
plots against Elizabeth, 36–38
Plymouth colony in America, 85–86
poem, Remember, remember,
    81–82, 138
polite pronouns, 97
Pope effigies at Bonfire Night, 77
Pope Leo X, 17
pronouns, first and third persons, 96
pronouns, second–person, 7
pronouns, second–person, 90–103
Protestants, 14, 27–28, 41
public thanksgiving, 69
Puritans, 26–27, 30, 41–42

Quakers, pronouns, 100–1

Raleigh, Sir Walter, 100
Recusant Catholics, 67, 79
recusants, 34, 41–42
Reformation Parliament, 21
Remember, remember (poem),
    81–82, 138
Restoration, 26–27
Ridolfi Plot, 37

search for plotters, 57, 58–60
search party, 50

Seven Sacraments Against Martin
    Luther, 15
Shakespeare's pronouns, 99
Sixtus V, Pope, S 36
Spanish alliance 11–12
Spanish Armada, 38
Spanish Brigade, 39
Spanish Treason, 39
Stafford Plot, 37
State Opening, 43, 46, 47, 48

tables of English personal pronouns, 94–96
thanksgiving church service, 69–70
thanksgiving, day of 66–67
"thou,": loss of, 91–103
Throckmorton Plot, 37
torture, 56–57

U.S. Constitution, Bill of Rights, 90

V for Vendetta, 138–40
vacancy in second–person plural pronouns, 103
villain becomes hero, 142
Virginia, 84–85

Wallace, Irving, 122
Warwickshire, 106
Washington, George, 88–89
Winthrop, Theodore, 108–9
Wintour, Thomas, 44

Y'all, 129–36
"yinz," 147
"you folks," 147
"you guys," 2–3, 7
"you people," 147
"yous," 147
"you–uns," 147
York, England, 123